F*CK YOU
Watch This.

TYLAR PAIGE

Say *F*ck You Watch This* & join me on social media.

IG @tylarpaige
TikTok @tylarpaige
FB /tylarpage

Share your FUWT story with hashtag #FUWatchThis

I respond to every message I receive as promptly as possible.

A story of lots of f*ckery and self-love discovery.

You won't. You can't. You shouldn't.

F*CK YOU
Watch This.

Tired of choosing the wrong men, she finally chose herself.

TYLAR PAIGE

For everyone who stayed by my side through all the fuckery.
Each of you have inspired me in ways I cannot express through words.

For everyone who left my side, you also inspired me.
But in ways I *can* express through words.

Fuck you, watch this.

And, for *me*.

You F*cking Ready?

I wasn't even hurt any more, I was just waiting for the shoe to drop. And boy, did it.

Why are you treating me like I'm disposable? I asked.

I'm your wife.

I saw the three dots in the little bubble, as John typed the final line that would end it all.

You've earned the title of disposable.

I was enraged at the audacity of this man to tell me this most horrific fucking thing you could ever say to a human being, even more so, your significant other. I packed my suitcase and booked a flight to Dallas for that night, then got the fuck out of there.

Finally, *for good.*

Table of Contents – The Fuckery that is…

1. A Bumpy Road
2. Childhood
3. The Stepdad
4. Bullies
5. High School
6. Dating
7. Loss
8. Engagement
9. A Destination Wedding
10. Photoshop
11. Stealing
12. A Fresh Start
13. Public Speaking
14. A Girls' Trip
15. The Truth
16. Gaslighting
17. Fingers and Toes
18. Narcissism
19. Deleting Texts
20. (Another) Fresh Start
21. Thanksgiving
22. Being Disposable
23. Butterflies
24. A Bachelor Party
25. The Grand Canyon
26. *Back to the Future*
27. New Year
28. 23 & Me
29. Destroying the Dress
30. COVID
31. No Work
32. A Kiss in the Rain
33. Fools Rush In
34. Rage
35. Getting Out
36. Dallas
37. A Psychopath

38. Harassment
39. Being Single on Purpose
40. New People
41. Cheating on Myself
42. Recommitting
43. Honesty
44. The Bucket List
45. Christmas
46. Not Being Kidnapped
47. Moza
48. A Hostel Party
49. Art
50. No Lights
51. A Motorcycle Ride
52. *The Neverending Story*
53. Going Home
54. Signs
55. A One-Night Stand
56. The Unknown
57. Not Fuckery

Foreword

By Josh Linkner

NEW YORK TIMES BESTSELLING AUTHOR
5X TECH ENTREPRENEUR
VENTURE CAPITAL INVESTOR

I first met Tylar back in 2009 when she was embarking upon founding her own creative marketing agency, which was quite a bold move in the middle of an economic crisis. Her tenacious attitude forged ahead, and she made it happen!

Knowing her personal story of overcoming challenges throughout her life, it's no surprise that this memoir is inspiring to readers who have experienced their own difficulties. Finding self-love through such a tumultuous journey takes courage and conviction, and once again, she made it happen.

As you read this book, you'll discover your own path to self-love while you resonate with Tylar's story. Anyone who's been through trauma, abuse, narcissism, or toxic relationships (be it romantic or familial) will benefit from her story.

Tylar is the type of woman who will always find success in her endeavors. She proves over and over that she can, she will, and she does – anything she puts her mind to do. Seeing her passion in writing this book, as well as her new fiction novel, Zwickel Station, makes me confident that authorhood is her true calling in life.

The Fuckery that is...

A Bumpy Road.

The Prologue

"Sometimes it's a bumpy road that leads to the most beautiful sights." – Ashley Abney

My name is Tylar, but most people call me Ty. I'm a creative advertising professional by day, a podcast host by night and a writer on the weekends. I have absolutely no filter and an exceptionally juvenile sense of humor – both useful traits for cutting through the bullshit and telling it like it is. Currently, I'm living in hot-as-fuck, sunny South Florida with Bula, my nine-year-old bulldog-boxer rescue pup who I'm convinced is my real soulmate.

I'm five-foot-seven weighing in at around 140 pounds (if I haven't eaten pizza for three days straight) and seem to have a talent for crossing state lines. I've been told I look like Jennifer Aniston, Julianne Hough, and Hayden Panettiere, among others I'm not quite sure I agree with.

I've also been involved in a whole lot of grade-A fuckery. Oh, the shit we do for "love".

***

It's a Saturday morning at a little café by the beach, not far from where I live. I've been single and loving life for over eight months now, focusing only on myself, my own journey, and my own happiness.

I can't deny that a small part of me wishes a gorgeous Paul-Walker-looking surfer guy will walk up to my table. He'll cast a shadow over me; and, in true Hollywood style, I'll turn to gaze up into his impossibly handsome face. Our eyes will meet, and *bam* – I'll fall, hard. Of course, he's your typical player type, so we'll spend months on an emotional rollercoaster before some ultimatum pushes him to confess his love. The tears will all be worth it when he tells me I'm the most beautiful girl in the world, inside and out, and we sail off into the sunset together to live happily ever after… right?

The fuck? That's such bullshit. Like a Katherine Heigl movie. Or that mushy *Save the Best for Last* bullshit #1 hit Vanessa Williams had back in the 90's.

Ugh. I've been waiting over thirty minutes for a refill of coffee in my fancy glass. Being by yourself at a café in Florida is like being a homeless person – not many people acknowledge you, because they think you don't have much to offer. The happy groups of tourists ordering brunch and drinking mimosas, or the "family that drinks together" hangover parties, around me are getting plenty of service. The staff are smiling, excusing their reaching over the table to refill drinks from bright glass pitchers, while I sit here with an empty cup.

Even a quick trip to the bathroom goes south quickly. When I report that the place's only female toilet is overflowing, the waitress' expression makes it clear she couldn't give less of a shit. And, with my lack of coffee evidently still at the bottom of the servers' priority list, I decide to leave – without paying $4.00 for the drink or leaving a tip, something exceptionally unusual for me.

I find a seat at a restaurant just a block away from the Shitty Service Café; and, since it's now noon, I order a mimosa at the bar. Swarms of people around me are drinking beer and watching college football.

I pull out my laptop, take a sip of my favorite cocktail, and start to write a prologue.

***

Everything that's happened in my life to get me to this point is, frankly, just fucked up. Don't get me wrong: I take responsibility for a lot of the things that have gone wrong. I'm pretty self-aware, and I'm always working to be a better version of myself. But this moment – right here, right now, when I sit down to write it all out? Even thinking about it makes me shit-scared. And I am not one to shy away from a great shit story.

As I put pen to paper (or, well, pixel to screen), I'm praying for strength, guidance, discipline, and motivation. I'm cognizant about making choices that'll keep me on a happy track, so that life continues to get better for me. I've worked tirelessly for over thirty years to overcome adversity, accept myself for who I am, and evolve into a self-loving person who acts on her core beliefs.

Learning to care for and love myself, in the same way that I care for and love others, is the hardest thing I have ever done. It's also been the most fulfilling, rewarding experience of my entire life.

We don't always act on our core beliefs – the ones we hold fast to and know to be true. Instead, we're prone to letting their more impetuous twins take hold of our minds. You know those thoughts you have, instantly, when you feel triggered? Say, if your boyfriend usually calls to say goodnight when you aren't together, but this one time, he doesn't? Your first, impulsive thought might be: *He's cheating on me.* You might even go into panic mode.

Your core belief, and what's most likely the truth, is that he's okay: he's probably just busy, or he fell asleep, or his phone decided to try out for the diving championship in a toilet and is now packed away taking a relaxing rice bath. But you act out of sorts on that impetuous belief, your mind racing away with thoughts like: *He has a laptop – he could send me a message through any social media platform. What is he doing? Is he ignoring me? Is his dick inside another woman? Is he lying dead in a ditch somewhere?*

Maybe he *is* a douchebag who's fucking someone else. It's not in your control. We can beat ourselves up for making the "wrong" choice – in that case, for choosing a guy who turned out to be a cheater – but there's no point in that. It'll only cause you pain in the long term.

Our core beliefs get tainted and twisted with all the crap we go through in life. From childhood trauma to the hurt we receive from strangers, coworkers, partners, friends, even family. It can feel impossible to start over with a new set of beliefs and values, purely focused on yourself and your happiness, especially after you've had your heart, mind, trust, or even body completely broken.

But you have a choice: to act on the impetuous belief, or act on the core belief. When you challenge the impetuous belief, you can form a new, core belief. It's much easier to obey once it's identified, and you start acting on it more and more, thereby taking control of your life. Throughout this book, I'll identify my own beliefs, actions, and most importantly, my challenges – new beliefs to counteract and change negative convictions – using my "BAC" model. Here's an example, featuring a self-affirming principle around which I've rebuilt my life.

Belief: Love isn't real unless it hurts you in some way.

Action: If you can change or "fix" someone, it will validate their love for you.

Challenge: No one who loves you will intentionally hurt you, period. You work hard enough in life, you don't need to work on a person, too.

When bullshit beliefs like this take form as thoughts, I like to envision them as nothing more than snowflakes inside a snow globe. I shake the shit out of the damn thing, watch those false beliefs swirl around with no direction and no purpose, then throw it at a huge tree and watch the glass shatter into a million pieces. The snowflakes fall into a river running below the tree, floating those snowflakes away and dissolving them. I think of the tree as my core belief, with all its strength, growth, experience, and stability.

The same holds true with anything negative that enters your mind.

—
5

Thoughts, feelings, fears, doubts… Picture that negative shit inside the globe, shake the fuck out of it, and toss it. Visualize this happening, and you will be amazed how quickly they leave you alone, creating room for positivity. For me, it magically just fucking works.

If you aren't someone who was ever presented with obstacles, challenges, or "holy shit, what the fuck do I do?!" kind of choices like I was, then you might not have ever had to say "fuck you, watch this" to someone. And that's great! Writing a book, based on my own experiences, that inspires other people to take action and control of their lives by fighting their toxic beliefs certainly wasn't my childhood dream. I wanted to write television commercials and emotionally evoking ad campaigns, and create artistic masterpieces with paint, charcoal, paper, and a camera (which, fortunately, I get to do in my adult life!).

Up until recently, I always believed that I needed a man to validate me. True love was the only thing I craved and *being* loved was the only way I could feel valuable. My identity was defined by how another person felt about me. I'd spent my entire life trying to replace the love I never received from my biological father, but doing this only attracted men who were just like him: absent, non-committal, emotionally unavailable. The good guys didn't stand a chance. I dismissed them all without a second thought, because there was no "work" to be done. I ended up equating "love" to pain, torture, and betrayal.

The people who say that they love you with words are supposed to show their love with actions, too – at least, 90%~ of the time. We all have moments when we fight, argue, say things we don't mean, and make mistakes. But when it comes to the dealbreaker-type shit – I'm talking about lying, cheating, stealing, causing physical pain, and whatever else you've decided isn't right for you in your love life – your partner should respect you enough to never, *ever* do those things.

If they don't, well, they should be the fuckery that is… the past.

I promise you, you can live without them, no matter how vehemently they might insist otherwise. You can, and you will. Break the cycle, say "fuck you, watch this," and go live your best life by yourself, for yourself.

The Fuckery that is...

Childhood.

"As children, it's a shame we don't get to create our own childhood. As adults, it's a privilege to create our own second childhood." – Ty Paige

I was born in Huntington, West Virginia to parents who didn't want me. I mean, they *kept* me, but it was always evident that I wasn't planned or a priority. I mean, shit – when my dad (who I'd only ever met twice after he left when I was three) died abruptly at just fifty-seven years old, all I got was a piss-poor, laminated eulogy bookmark, accompanied by a letter from my stepmom, a woman I didn't even know. I wish I had blocked that shitty excuse for consolation from my mind, but I recall it saying something like "Your dad thought of you often". Really? Because my name wasn't even spelled right in his obituary. Strangers often spell my name Tyler instead of Tylar, but c'mon. And why the fuck was it even in there? He didn't know me at all. I was never part of his life, so why was I forced to be part of his death?

My mother, meanwhile, would often call me a "cong-u-nong-tong" – which, at about age eleven, I figured out was code for *cunt*. She'd often use words like that, deriving from this secret language she'd invented with her high school friend they called "double Chinese". Basically, you just added "ong" to any consonant, then said any vowels that came between them normally.

It was pretty simple, really, but I guess not so simple that any average kid could figure it out. That was probably the biggest downside to being smart as shit from an early age – working out how to spell this ugly-sounding word she called me, but having no clue what it meant. I did have a shred of innocence left, despite knowing a lot of other unsavory terms like *fuck* (thank the pedophile my mom married, after my dad left us when I was three, for that one). More on that depressing-as-fuck saga in the next chapter.

"I never wanted kids! I never wanted to love anyone more than I love myself!" seemed like one of my mother's favorite things to tell us kids. If that didn't hammer home what I'd long since been acutely aware of, I once had the unenviable pleasure of hearing the story of how she'd driven from our hometown all the way to Michigan to find an abortion clinic and kill me off. Real nice, Mom.

Despite all this, I don't believe my mother was a truly *bad* person – really, she had several more positive qualities, showed love and concern in her own way. But she wasn't cut out for motherhood.

School didn't provide any respite, either. I was bullied relentlessly in elementary for things like being "poor" and "ugly". I vividly remember recess in second grade, where I'd climb inside one of those big colorful tires to avoid my schoolmates' nasty comments. And, as if this wasn't enough fuckery, I had an extra reason to dread going home every day.

The Fuckery that is...

The Stepdad.

"Never let the past define your future." – Ty Paige

Mom brought a man home when I was about four years old. I won't even hide his name: Joe Miller.

Joe was asleep in her bed the first time I saw him. It was the middle of the night, and I'd gone to my mom's room because I was having bad dreams. I remember thinking he must have been Native American, since his dark beige, reddish-tanned skin had such a resemblance to the depictions of Native American people I'd encountered in schoolbooks and some old cartoons.

I ran out of her room screaming, "Mommy, mommy, there's an Indian sleeping in your bed!" Mom was crashed out on the couch; but she woke up and comforted me, and I eventually fell back asleep. Little did I know, then, that I was right to be worried about this strange man, because this was just the beginning of six or so years of *hell*.

Every day, when I walked the three quarters of a mile home from school, I'd look down and count the cracks in the sidewalks. Each one meant getting closer to a house of horrors, a few less seconds before I'd once again be subjected to Joe holding me hostage indoors while Mom was at work and my sister played outside with her friends. My mother would later insinuate that I was to blame for the sexual abuse. Apparently, my five-year-old self had made her feel bad when I asked her, "Is he going to be my new daddy?", and she'd been *compelled* to stay with him.

You know those so-called "formative years" we're taught about as adults? My own were filled with abuse, abandonment, and rejection; and I learned those things were pretty much all I was good for. I sat on the couches of several therapists who told me I needed to associate with "that little girl" – but I always told them, "Fuck that." I didn't want to relive the abuse, and especially not the confusion that came along with it. Even nowadays, if ever I speak of what I went through as a kid, it's as if I'm just painting a picture of an entirely unrelated girl who had *this* or *that* happen to her. Why, you ask? Because those things did not happen to *me*.

I know who "that little girl", all too often, grows up to be. I've created standards for myself that don't align with those expectations, the ways society (and often science) says the child with the shitty upbringing "should" turn out, and they've helped to shape me into the woman I am today. I'm successful, fun, outgoing, personable… In a way, it's like I cloned and made an upgraded version of myself, who decided, from the moment she came into the world, that a bad childhood wouldn't stop her from having a good life.

We finally left Joe when I was just shy of ten years old, secretly moving a few states away. It was a chance to start over, a promise of a life completely removed from all the bullshit. I focused on that with every last bit of my being. A new neighborhood, a new school where I'd make new friends, the chance to become an entirely different person. I was determined: *this* Ty was going to be popular, and pretty – and she was never going to look back.

The Fuckery that is...

Bullies.

"The coconut is a symbol of resilience. Even in the conditions where there's very little nourishment and even less nurturance, it flourishes, growing taller than most of the plants around it. Be a coconut." – Unknown

The first couple years of my shiny, new life in South Carolina were everything I'd dreamed they would be. I had great friends, and I was well-known and well-liked. In sixth grade, I even had boys that wanted to "go with me". Mom's new boyfriend, Bill, was well-off, since he owned a construction fabric company in neighboring Charlotte, North Carolina; and he'd buy me things that made me appear to live an attractive, middle-class lifestyle. I wouldn't say I was one of the most popular girls in school, but I kept up with the "in-crowd" pretty well.

The summer I turned 12, I went to see the movie *Ghost* – you know, the one where Patrick Swayze plays a spirit trying to save his still-living girlfriend from a money-laundering murderer. I was obsessed with Demi Moore's character, and I decided I wanted my hair to be just like hers. So, I headed to the mall with my friend Becca, found one of those budget haircut places, and declared my wish to the hairdresser. In less than thirty minutes, she was done. She'd chopped off my light brown hair all the way up to my ears, creating a style that resembled a bowl cut with a feminine touch. I adored it.

I don't recall my mother or my sister making any comments at all about my new hairstyle. Even though we'd moved somewhere far away, far from all the shit I'd suffered for a decade, there was one thing that hadn't changed: my near invisibility to everyone in my immediate family. It explains why I spent so much time around my friends and their folks, and why, as an adult, I'd end up dependent on my social life for validation.

***

The three months of carefree fun came to an end before I knew it, signaled by the annual back-to-school rush splashed all over the media. Most kids might groan at the thought of going back to sitting in stuffy classrooms – but I had a special reason to be anxious to get that year's schedule. I had the *biggest* crush on a guy named Chad, and I was praying I'd be with him in as many classes as possible!

The first day of school started out pretty normally. I walked in, found my locker, decorated it from top to bottom so it yelled, "This is Ty's space!" to everyone who walked by. I met up with Becca and Kara, another one of my close friends, and we walked down the hall together.

Then we saw the popular kids making faces at us.
I tried to say hi to one of the girls, but she completely ignored me. The same thing happened with several of the other kids; and I was left feeling totally confused and awkward until third period, when

---

I found out they were all making fun of me behind my back. They'd even given me a nickname, "Sinéad", comparing my beloved trim to the singer's practically shaved head.

I asked my teacher for a bathroom pass and locked myself in a stall to cry. Would Chad jump on the Sinéad bandwagon? I worried as I sobbed. Would he even *look* at me anymore? Was I doomed to forever be "the girl with the bad haircut", always teased and tormented while the perfect Marys, Christines, and Katies paraded through the halls with their long, flowing hair and skyscraper bangs?

Fortunately, Becca and Kara never once left my side, no matter what horrible comments the bullies threw at me, or at them for daring to still hang out with me. As for Chad, he and I eventually became friends, and he'd even flirt a little when we chatted over the phone in the evenings. But he never gave me the time of day at school – if any of his friends in the popular crowd found out that we so much as talked, it would destroy his reputation (which, as we all know, is *everything* in middle school). So, we kept a secret friendship all through seventh grade.

At least once a week, I wept when I got home.

***

At the ripe old age of 12, I certainly didn't have the emotional intelligence to form a BAC (Belief – Action – Challenge). But now I do; and I've made one in retrospect.

Belief: If you aren't just like everyone else, no one will like you.

Action: Keep your hair long, your clothes tidy, and your personality like that of the other girls.

Challenge: We were not born to be anyone other than ourselves. Kids are mean. Kids are harsh. Kids don't understand that differences are what make us unique and special. As time goes on, and the world evolves into a loving, supportive, and encouraging community, everyone will be accepted for who they are – much more so than when you were stuck in middle school.

***

After the social disaster that was seventh grade, there was no way in hell I was keeping my hair short, no matter how much I loved it. I went into 8th grade having somewhat "redeemed" my looks in the eyes of my classmates, and they stopped being so harsh – although one kid, Jeremy, would still try to rally up the bully crowds by calling me "Sinéad" whenever I was called on by the teacher. Really, he was just embarrassing himself more than anything. And honestly, he probably just had a crush on me.

My last year of middle school was kind of a breeze by comparison. I had a group of good friends I rode the bus with, including Kara and Becca, and together we'd become a sort of little clique I felt like I belonged with. With their company, I managed to survive the last few months, and I was ready for the next chapter of life – high school.

The Fuckery that is...

High School.

"Tell me and I forget. Teach me and I remember. Involve me and I learn". – Benjamin Franklin

My high school, while still technically in South Carolina, was situated in bumfuck nowhere. I don't know if that had any bearing on a lot of my classmates being less than well-behaved, but my mostly decent conduct became yet another reason I stood out (although this time, thank God, they didn't bully me for it).

I soon realized that being book smart was never going to be my thing. Not that I was dumb – far from it! I was top of the class when it came to common sense and "street smarts", and I was just way more interested in writing, designing, and teaching myself Adobe programs.

For all the four years of high school, my teachers insisted, "She has potential," or, "If she would just apply herself, her grades would be better." But once I got to a point where I *thought* I was smarter than most of them, I hated school.

I was the super-ambitious type; a self-starter who just wanted to do what I knew I was good at and skip the shit that I *thought* would never matter in life. I wanted to let my creative beast free! I didn't give a fuck about biology, or chemistry, or physics. History? I wanted to go and *make* it, not sit there memorizing facts about the Civil War!

Deep down, though, I knew I needed to do the work I absolutely *had* to do. I poured the rest of my time into cheerleading, editing the school newspaper and yearbook, presiding over the Students Against Drunk Driving association, and serving on the student council. I seemed to have a promising future, even being a C-student – and, to top it off, I was *everyone's* friend. I'm serious! I bet you couldn't track down a single person I went to high school with that would say anything else.

My weekends were usually filled with friends and activities that were a little at odds with the image my in-school persona might suggest. Even though some of my buddies lived over 20 fucking miles away, we made it work!

I was known to be fun-loving and outgoing, to throw back some beers at field parties, or perhaps chug some Boone's Farm straight from the bottle (because that's how it's done when you're not fancy!). I dated the cute, popular football and soccer player for over two years. I'd lie to my mom occasionally about where I was going or what I was doing. All in all, I was a typical teen – except, perhaps, when it came to my home life.

***

It was a Wednesday night in fall. I was in 12th grade, and a friend was driving me home from chorus practice. I will never

understand why the fuck someone allowed me to be in chorus – I am, categorically, the *worst* singer in the entire world. You can ask any of my friends who've witnessed me sing karaoke.

Anyway: I got home, went inside, and saw my mother lying on the kitchen floor in a puddle of her own piss. I immediately thought she was dead. They don't show you in movies that you usually soil yourself when you die, because the fluids need to exit your body.

Aside from weird bits of trivia like that, Mom's work as a nurse had armed me with the knowledge of how to do a lot of minor medical-related things. I went over to her and checked her pulse. She was alive, but incoherent. I looked around the kitchen and spied an empty pill bottle, nested beside a near-empty bottle of – I couldn't be sure, maybe vodka or rum? I didn't drink much alcohol other than the shitty beers or cheap wine I already mentioned, so I wasn't familiar with any hard liquors.

My older sister had moved out when I was in 11th grade, so it was now just me and Mom. I wrapped her arms around my neck, picked her up, and carried her to her bedroom, which fortunately was right next to the kitchen. It wasn't easy, even with my 135-pound athletic, cheerleader build. I was only used to lifting up girls who could tighten their muscles to become lighter, not 145 pounds of dead weight.

Once I got her into bed, Mom mumbled a few things that made zero sense to me.

"What's hurting you, Mom?" I asked.

I'll never forget her reply. Every time I think about it, it stabs me from one side of my stomach through to the other, piercing every organ in between.

She drunkenly slurred, *"You."*

***

Looking back, I'm not entirely sure why my mother thought I was so bad. I knew better than to tell lies, but I was 17, and if I wanted to go and get drunk with my friends in a field, was I really going to tell her that? Not after what my sister did to her. She'd get right in Mom's face and tell her to fuck off, she was going to do whatever she wanted. I always saw how much that upset Mom, so I decided that lying would be the easier route. What she didn't know wouldn't hurt her, right? For the record: I'm not dismissing lying. It was wrong of me to lie on the occasions when I did. But was it *really* so terrible that it made her want to die?

In that moment, I had my very first real-time BAC – one that would end up tainting my ideas of love throughout my life. As a type-A person who loves to be in control, it made sense at the time.

Belief: Love is supposed to hurt.

Action: You lied, that hurt her. She tried to take her life because of it, that hurt you.

Challenge: Keep your head up, keep your confidence. You can work to make things right for you both.

This might well have been the challenge that laid the foundation for my future belief that I'd always have to "work" on someone else, to try and "fix" them, for it to be real love. A family is supposed to provide you with real, unconditional love; but there I was, already associating love with pain.

I know now that my real-time challenge was false. As with anything in life, we don't always have the right answer at the right time.

***

My high-school boyfriend and I had just broken up a couple months before the mom incident. He'd had a little fling with one of my closest friends while on a church youth group trip, and it broke my heart. However, I will give him *ultimate* kudos for telling me about it, not covering it up or lying. You'd think, after we'd spent most of our teen years together, this would have destroyed my ability to trust. But it didn't. I was still hopeful that I'd one day meet a guy who would be my soulmate, and we'd have that oh-so-perfect happily ever after that we see in movies.

Fuck. I could not have been more wrong.

The Fuckery that is...

Dating.

"First impressions are bullshit. Anyone can say anything. Don't believe anyone is who they say they are. Wait until they show you." – Ty Paige

It was a beautiful day in June 2016. By this time, I was living just outside of Detroit. I had tickets to a Detroit Tigers game, and was supposed to be meeting my best friend, Sue, to drive downtown to the stadium together. She bailed on me at the last minute; but me being the independent type, I said, "screw it" and went alone. I already knew a few of our other friends would be there, I just wouldn't be able to sit with them. Plus, Comerica Park has an awesome Pepsi party porch that overlooks the field. Why the fuck would I want to miss out on that?

Cut to a little while later. I was walking around the massive, open-air porch, beer in hand, by myself. I reached into my purse and caught my finger on something sharp. I dug down to pull it out. It was a brown cocktail-stirring stick with a pirate head on top that I'd snagged from this snazzy little themed bar in San Francisco earlier that year.

I stood there staring at it for a moment, thinking it must have been lying at the bottom of that purse for months. Then, it happened.

A shadow fell over me; and, of course, I looked up. I found myself staring up into a set of eyes that could melt you into them if you couldn't tear your own gaze away. The same golden-brown, speckled circus color of peanut butter that you can damn near taste just by smelling. Or, in this case, looking.

He was over six feet tall with an athletic 200-plus pound build. His skin was a perfect tone of tan, and he had this mysterious glow, making you feel warm inside without warning…

"Are you going to start stabbing people with that?" he said casually to me, who was standing there speechless, still holding that stupid pirate drink stick.

Let's just say that if I was planning to go on a stabbing spree, he was the type of guy who could make you change your mind about *anything and everything*. His effortless charm, his wit, his looks – they'd make a person about to jump off the Empire State Building run straight to the firefighters and help them save kittens instead.

Here he is, I thought. *The one I've been waiting for.*

***

The mystery man – John – told me it'd be a week and a half before we could get together, since he was going to be super busy. But as we texted more, that window, somehow, got smaller and smaller. When I mentioned having VIP access to a fireworks show that coming Monday, he was suddenly available; and on the Sunday, just four days after meeting, we went on our first date.

We sat at a Bloody Mary bar in downtown Detroit for a couple hours, sipping cocktails and chatting it up. He told me he was from a small town in a southernmost state, worked in corporate America, and had a daughter about to head off to college. He'd just moved to the Detroit area a few months prior and had made some friends through work.

Neither of us wanted the good times to end, so we continued on to the next bar for a beer.

About twelve hours later, I said goodnight to John, kissed him, and went home. We ended up seeing each other almost every night the next week; and, once I felt comfortable, I joined him at his house for a game night along with his two friends, Ethan and Jen, who were passing through.

Since John had overnight guests, I didn't expect to sleep with him that night – I mean, who wants to think about their buddy and his date doing it in the same house where they're staying? The idea made me kind of nervous, too. I liked him – *really* liked him – and I didn't want to ruin things by going too fast. Plus, he definitely seemed like the type of guy who could get any girl he wanted into bed with him. If I was just another one of those girls, I wouldn't be special… But we did end up sleeping together, and I got all the feels, like "oh shit, he's going to be long term!"

***

Over the next day, I got several texts from John. I didn't want him to feel bad or like I was ignoring him, so I reluctantly invited him to play volleyball with me that night (it was a Friday). He said he couldn't because he had to work late. No problem – I'd pulled a lot of overtime myself as an entrepreneur. If John needed to stay at the office for a few extra hours, that was totally understandable.

8:00 PM. I was taking a break between volleyball games, just scrolling through Facebook. I used to keep the Nearby Friends thing turned on, probably from some sort of mid-thirties fear of missing out (FOMO, as millennials call it). I got a notification that John was nearby.

Considering his work and home were both a good 30 minutes from me, this was interesting, to say the least. I waited a bit, then texted him, thinking to catch him in a possible lie.

Me: Hey, how's work going?

John: Got a text from a friend this afternoon and said screw work, she wanted to take me out for birthday drinks!

Me: Oh fun, have a good time!

John: What are you doing?

Me: I'm at volleyball still. Heading home soon.

Nothing red-flag-ish about any of that, except... when I'd asked him to come play volleyball, it had been closer to evening. The timing was off. And why hadn't he just told me that his friend asked to meet up? *He's lying,* my gut told me.

Always believe your gut feeling.

The truth, as I'd eventually find out, was that John was on a date with another girl. We'd just spent, oh, I don't know, seven or eight days together… and he was seeing someone else *the night after we first had sex?*

He tried to come over that night. I said no, my intuition already telling me that this wasn't some innocent birthday get-together he was having. Keep in mind, he'd only lived here a few short months, and he'd made no secret of the fact he'd used multiple dating apps. Again, that was no problem in itself – but when you start getting more serious with someone (ahem, me), it's time to shut down the other potential partners. We'd never talked about having an open relationship, and I certainly didn't want one.

***

The next day, John took me out for a day date. We spent the whole weekend together, even inviting our friends to join us at the pool. We all had a blast, everything was great, and I almost forgot about those suspicious texts. *Almost.*

It was a few weeks later when I caught him messaging Amanda.

I know a great activity that helps reduce stress

Is the text she'd sent him. Likely *not* referring to mountain climbing.

For fuck's sake, right in front of me? I confronted John about it. He lied, claiming Amanda had shown interest in him at one point, but he'd shut her down and they agreed to remain friends.

Whatever. I let it go; but another week went by, and I was severely suffering "down there"– shit, I'm not supposed to have a filter! My *vagina* hurt so bad. Something was wrong. *Really* wrong.

Now, John was very well-endowed, so I thought maybe he'd just torn me. Either way, I went to the gynecologist and, sure enough, I had fucking chlamydia. I'd never had an STD before, and I hadn't been with anyone in over six months before I met John. He insisted he was clean – he hadn't had sex since March, myself not included, and he'd been tested in May – but I knew better.

Finding Amanda on social media was way too easy, since I'd seen her last name on his phone. As I semi-stalked her Facebook just before I sent her a message, I thought, *nah, he wouldn't fuck her*.

Boy, was I wrong. Turned out John didn't discriminate, by size or looks, when it came to fuckbuddies. Now, I know so many amazing, drop-dead-gorgeous, plus-size women; and, frankly, I think *every* woman is beautiful in her own way. But since I'd lost about 45 pounds a few years prior, John's messing around with Amanda, when he was supposed to be *my* partner, made me feel like all the work I'd done to get healthy and toned was pointless.

Anyway, I messaged Amanda, asking her when was the last time she and John slept together. She didn't respond – at least, not directly. She *did* text John, demanding that he tell his girlfriend to leave her alone, along with some variety of "fuck off." Even with this pretty damning evidence, John still pretended as if they had nothing more than a platonic friendship. Yeah, right. No guy friend of mine would ever tell me to "fuck off" if we really were just friends.

It took almost two months to get John to fess up to his sexual relationship with Amanda. Of course, he had me believing it all happened *before* he met me, and that she wouldn't stop trying to keep something going. I'd find out in 2019, once I'd left him, that they had an intimate relationship extending well into ours. Thank you, Amanda, for being honest only *after* I married and divorced him. Then again, if she'd told me we were sharing a STD vehicle way back when, I guess I wouldn't have a book to write. I'd also have a lot more success, money, and sanity, but that's beside the point.

* * *

August. John invited me to Texas to meet his family, including his daughter who was moving into college. Of course, I said yes.

And, of *course*, he'd made plans to see an old fuck buddy during his Denver layover. I asked him about their exchange, and he lied again. She'd told him she couldn't make it, he claimed, because she had to go see a friend out of town that night.

Bullshit. I saw the message. He told her that his plans changed, and he no longer had a layover.

Why, oh dear God *why*, couldn't this man just be honest and tell her, "Hey, I have a girlfriend now, this isn't appropriate"? Did he need to keep her in his back pocket *just in case?* She lived across the damn country! It's not like she was an hour away, and they could get together for some sport sex whenever they pleased. Why was I not enough for him?

Good grief. Maybe the pussy was just that good.

He'd also been texting Nicole, some girl from his hometown. This one was a little weird. I'd never heard her name before, and one day when we were driving to volleyball, he just started telling me about a girl he dated for a while right before he moved to Detroit. She was "model gorgeous", but crazy. They were apparently still cordial, still friends. No problem, I figured. He wouldn't have

———

wanted to stay with someone unstable, but that didn't mean friendship was off the table.

I get that, you know. I'm not so insecure that a potential partner having an ex or previous fling still in his life is an issue. Shit, one of my best guy friends, Josh, is someone I used to hook up with. We've been friends for over ten years, now. We've always had some wild things going on life, so we were never a good match for anything other than the month-long series of one night stands we had. But at least I was upfront and honest with John about it.

***

Fast forward a month. I'm getting ready to leave town for a weekend with my best friend, Sue, and I see he's getting late-night and early-morning texts from Nicole. I had to ask him, because the timing of those messages was weird, and I ended up reading them. They were flirty little *goodnight, good morning,* and *stay sexy* types of texts.

Well, that's fucking inappropriate.

I called John out on it. He'd even invited her to fly up from Houston for the weekend while I was going to be out of town! His reply? "I was just joking, she knows that."

I didn't know this at the time, but John was my first true experience with a narcissist. A huge trait of narcissism involves gaslighting – making you question your reality – and turning anything you find offensive into a "joke". People with this personality disorder also like to tell you that you're "crazy" when you're completely within your rights to be pissed off or upset. I later suspected this was the root of John's description of Nicole.

After witnessing a few of John's flirtatious interactions with other women, I had a chat with him.

"If you're going to communicate like this with other girls, then you're going to lose me," I stated. "I hear you when you say you don't want to hurt their feelings, but *my* feelings should matter more to you now that we're together, and you're telling me you love me."

"Okay, Ty," he conceded. "You're right. I'll be more careful about how I speak to them."

Phew. That felt like a little win.

***

The BAC moment arrived, and it looked like this:

Belief: If a man changes for you, it means he loves you.

Action: Basically, you must coach a man on how to treat you right in a relationship.

Challenge: No, fuck that. No man who loves you will talk to other women inappropriately. A good man will make other women jealous of you, not you jealous of other women.

***

A few more suspicious things happened over the next several months - but John had said he'd re-evaluate how he communicated with other women, whether they were past romantic or sexual interests, colleagues, friends, etc., and I wanted to trust him. So, I ignored most of it. I'd question him occasionally about specific texts he'd get late on, or when he'd hide his phone, but I was working to believe that he was the "good guy" everyone saw.

When he told me that he and his ex of nine years, Grace, broke up because she hated his daughter, I believed it. When he told me they were still "best friends" – so much so that she and her fiancé had asked John to attend their wedding – I thought that was strange, but I had no reason not to think it was true. After all, she had moved on, and seemed much happier in her new relationship.

Despite all his faults, I truly thought John *was* a good guy, albeit with some rough edges. He seemed to love and care about me, though I'd later come to find out all this attention this was nothing more than love-bombing – showering me with affection, holding my attention so he could lure me in, keep me as nothing more than a pretty prop in the stage play of his life.

The Fuckery that is...

Loss.

"If you plan on showing up for my funeral, you better show up for my life." – Ty Paige

John and I spent nearly every day together for almost seven months, and our separate leases were both up in January 2017. So, in mid-December, we decided to move in together.

The first house we looked at was a colonial four-bedroom, two-and-a-half-bath home on a dead-end street in Farmington Hills. It was situated just two blocks away from a main road, less than a mile from the shopping centers, and only about half a mile from the freeway. We met with the owners, Henry and Cindy, and immediately felt like we'd made new friends. Within just a couple days, we were signing the lease and scheduling our move-in date. Everything seemed perfect.

***

January 11, 2017. 8:12 PM. Since we weren't due to relocate until the end of the month, I was still living in my Royal Oak townhouse. John was lying on the couch watching TV, while I was in my basement art studio working on a new painting. A text came through from my client and friend, Steve.

Steve: Hey, Ty. Call me when you get this. It's urgent.

I responded right away, thinking it must be work-related.

Me: Hey Steve! Can it wait until tomorrow morning?

Steve: No.

What could be so pressing that he needed to talk to me *now*? Why did he sound so… off?

I headed upstairs and stepped outside to call him.

"Hey, Ty."

"Hey. What's going on? Everything okay?"

"No, Ty. It's Adam."

Adam was my best guy friend. I'd met him back in 2008 while watching football at a local bar, and we'd clicked instantly. He was a year older than me, so I'd always joked that he was like my big brother. He was well-known and loved from Detroit, throughout every suburb and city, all the way to Chicago. A Michigan State alumnus and Detroit entrepreneur, he always introduced me and my business to as many of his associates as possible. He'd always believed in me. We'd traveled together to national football championship games; partied together; worked together; attended basketball, hockey, and football games. His entire immediate family considered me one of their own.

***

I remember one night, when Adam left his credit card and driver's license in a taxi he'd taken. We hadn't even been hanging out together; but, later that evening, I ended up taking the same taxi from Detroit to Royal Oak. When I got in the cab and told the driver where I was going, he said, "Perfect! I need to return a license and credit card there, anyway." He flashed the license briefly at me.

"That's my friend Adam's!" I said. "Let me call him real quick."

I asked Adam if it was okay for the driver to give me the cards – I'd drop them off at Adam's place later – and he was over the moon.

"Take my card tonight. Drinks on me for getting it back!"

***

Over the past few years, mine and Adam's friendship had taken on an extra dimension. We'd been working together in a client/agency capacity, at the company that Adam and his dad owned together, and at which Steve was the chief operations officer.

"Is he okay?" I asked Steve. "What happened?"

"We found him today. He… passed away."

Steve's voice was shaky, and I immediately felt my heart drop into my stomach. Adam and I were supposed to have lunch the next day. Was this some sick joke? He couldn't be for real. Surely…

———

Steve went on, telling me all the details they had at this point. I was the first non-family member they called. *Shit*. I'd have to call all our mutual friends and be *that* person. Fuck.

I hung up the phone, walked inside and sat on the first step of my townhouse's hardwood stairs.

Adam was only thirty-eight years old.

I started bawling. John, still lying on the couch, asked me what was wrong. When I managed to get the breath to tell him, he came over nonchalantly and wrapped his arms around me. It didn't feel genuine at all, but I took it for what it was worth: a warm body to hold me and comfort me as I sat there, in shock, for almost an hour.

***

The next two weeks, I was preoccupied with packing and getting ready to move to our new house. Adam's family had decided to delay the funeral until later in the month, so I could help with the memorial, service, and memory boards.

I finished moving on Sunday. The ceremony was the next day – and John left town for work right after. Leaving me, all alone, in this huge house, rocked to my core after saying a final goodbye to my brother's ashes.

When John returned, I decided, we had to have a talk.

***

John had just moved his stuff in, and was, once again, sitting on a couch – his own, which we'd decided would go next to mine.

"You know," I began. "I just don't feel like I'm a priority. I know work is important, but do you realize I just lost one of my best friends, who was like my brother? You aren't acting like my feelings are important."

"I– I know. I don't know. You *are* more important than work, I'm sorry."

"Work will always be there. Look at what just happened! *I* may not always be here. I need to know I matter to you."

John teared up – one of only two times he'd do so in my presence. "I'll make sure of it. You *are* my priority, Ty."

He got up and went upstairs, with a slight delay between each step, telling me he just needed a few minutes alone. I was on my way out the door anyway, so I said I'd see him later.

I got in my car and let out a sigh of relief. It seemed as if just talking to him was going to make everything better – and I had a brief BAC moment.

Belief: Communicating feelings will always make things better.

Action: Stand up for yourself and your feelings, and never make someone try to read your mind.

Challenge: When someone shows you who they really are, believe them. Actions speak louder than words.

The Fuckery that is...

Engagement.

"Roses are red, violets are blue. Flowers die, and this love will, too." – Ty Paige

The next few months breezed by. I was craving a vacation in March, so I booked a cruise for us to take right around St. Patrick's Day. On board, we met two other couples, who lived in Florida, and ended up hanging out with them the entire week. One of the couples, a pair from Michigan named Maggie and Tom, would stay good friends of ours for a long while after.

***

Our place had become the central location for parties, since we had a huge house and backyard with a two-story deck and a volleyball court. As the warmer weather approached, we decided to have a big "Welcome Summer" bash. I'd introduced John to all of my friends, who took to him instantly – largely thanks to his effortless charm and narcissistic tendency to always try and fit it with anyone he was around.

Naturally, we invited everyone we knew, most of whom had been close with me long before John was ever a part of my life. A handful of people John worked with showed up, as well. We set up backyard games like cornhole and ladder golf, busted out the hot dog roller I'd scored from a bodega in Mackinac Island, grilled up delicious meats and appetizers, and offered up tons of beer. It was June 3rd.

By about 8:00 PM, there were at least fifty people hanging out, eating, drinking, and socializing. Sue grabbed me and asked if we could talk in private; so, we made our way to the front of the house. She told me about a personal issue that she hadn't had a chance to discuss with me, though she insisted everything was okay.

As we chatted, a car carrying a few more of our friends pulled up to park, and I ran out to greet them. We stood in the street for a few minutes, until we were interrupted by Sue yelling:

"Ty! Come on, we've gotta get back!"

I didn't think much of it – we *were* missing a pretty awesome party, after all. We all went back to the yard; and, as I rounded the corner by the first level of the deck, I saw John standing there with a single red rose.

I hate red roses. He should have known that. They are so cliché.

Everyone else was waiting on the deck, eyes fixed on us in anticipation, as if we were the stars of some big-budget stage show. My friends (and those *friends* who are no longer so due to believing John's lies) had a front row seat to Act One of what would be the best theatrical experience they'd ever have the *joy* of witnessing.

I cupped my hand around my mouth in disbelief and walked up to him. He gave me a pretty pathetic proposal, something like:

"I want to make you happy for once. Will you marry me?"

We'd pretty much determined that we would get married someday, so I guess I just settled for this pitiful attempt to be romantic.

"Of course!" was my answer as I crouched over and hugged him.

The congratulations and celebrations lasted all night – I don't think we went to sleep until after 5:00 AM. We did have accommodations for about twelve people, and always welcomed anyone who'd been drinking to spend the night, so several of our guests ended up staying over.

I woke up with that giddy feeling still rushing around my body. Holy shit – I was *engaged!*

***

I spent the next eight months planning everything myself. I even planned the bridal shower that my friends insisted on throwing for me. I had no idea what I could possibly need at thirty-eight years old that I didn't already have; but I went along with it, mostly for the sake of getting together with all my gal pals, dressing up, drinking mimosas, and celebrating *me*. It was nice to have something to look forward to, and to take my mind off whatever John was doing at his bachelor party that same weekend in Scottsdale, Arizona.

My bachelorette party was just two weeks before the wedding. My friends did a wonderful job planning everything with such sparkle. We started the night with appetizers and cocktails at a local bar, and I'd gone outside for some fresh air, and happened to look across the street.

What the fuck was John doing at the bar right across the street? I mean, could you imagine how pissed he would have been if I'd flown to Arizona and stood outside the club where he was with his friends at his bachelor party? If I had, I would've witnessed what is likely not a spoiler warning by now – him with a few women, and a whole lot of fucking.

I walked over and said hi to him and his friends. He asked if I was having a good time, to which, of course I was. But his appearance was not necessarily one I expected, or desired. They left to continue a night of bar hopping, and I went back to my chugging drinks and dancing with my girls for the rest of the night.

***

Before I knew it, our destination wedding in Cancun was just around the corner. I packed up two large suitcases filled with "John and Ty" wedding favors, bouquets, hot pink robes, lots of extra makeup, hair accessories – and, of course, my dress, which I'd flown to New York City to buy from none other than Kleinfeld.

In our matching kelly-green bride and groom T-shirts, we flew off to Mexico.

The Fuckery that is...

A Destination Wedding.

"When someone shows you who they are, believe them."
– Maya Angelou

Sunday marked the start of seven days at an all-inclusive resort, for which I'd already paid the full price of the stay, and the 50% deposit for our wedding package for 65 guests. Of those 65, only two had booked the trip for the same length of time: Henry and Cindy, our landlords-turned-friends. Almost all the other guests would arrive on Tuesday for a five-day vacation, with some arriving as late as Thursday. Our wedding itself was on Friday, so we wanted to make sure everyone could make it while also giving them time to have fun of their own. As our friends and families trickled in throughout the week, we went out to the resort's clubs and bars, ate delicious breakfasts and lunches, kicked back with drinks by the pool, and arranged dinners at the best restaurants.

That Wednesday, we were all hanging out by the water – a daily ritual for us, by now – playing pool volleyball, mingling, and trying to ignore the random people who seemed to be hanging around us or shooting us glances when they thought we weren't looking.

Little did we know, when John's brother and his wife arrived that afternoon, one of the concierges had overheard him talking on the phone while he was checking in. You see, he was a well-respected sports medicine doctor, and one mention of the Dallas Cowboys from him started a rumor that some of the players were staying at the resort!

Anyway, we'd also planned to have our final bachelor and bachelorette parties in the evening: separate to start, then joining forces later. Before venturing outside the resort to really start the celebrations, we all went to dinner as a huge group. I'd had a few novelty daiquiris at the pool earlier, which hadn't affected me at all, and I'd never been so ready to down a beer and get in the party mood.

I was only about halfway through my first beer when I felt the overwhelming panic.

I knew I had to get out of there as fast as possible. It was only going to be a matter of minutes before I had a full-blown anxiety attack. I told the group I wasn't feeling well, told John I was going turn in for the night.

"Just go on out tonight without me," I said to John as I stood up to go. "And have so much fun!"

One of my bridesmaids offered to come with me to settle me into my room. I changed out of my spaghetti strapped keyhole white dress I'd bought just for this occasion, and into my pajamas. I curled up under the blanket and spent hours trying to breathe and calm myself down. I had no idea what sparked this panic inside me – perhaps it was spending the whole day in the sun, mixed with the tiny bit of liquor in my daiquiris? I didn't know.

If you've ever had a panic attack, you know how impossible it is to relax, let alone sleep. I think I slept a total of about an hour, in short increments of about 10-15 minutes.

***

Around 4:30 AM, I was still alone. I hadn't heard anything from him at all, not even a quick text to check on me. I had a WTF moment. I knew the resort had a taco bar that was open 24/7, but the group had gone out into the city to party; and surely, if they were back, he would have let me know.

I sent him a text.

Me: Hey, it's almost 5 am, where are you?

John: Hanging out with the group up at Paco's Taco, you know, I never really get to see them.

Me: When are you coming back?

John: In a bit, don't worry.

Another hour later, John strolled in, drunk off his ass.

I looked at him, discontent clear on my face.

"We have to be up in an hour to catch the shuttle to the catamaran," I reminded him.

He fell fast asleep, and I lay there realizing that this was such bullshit. I didn't want to be mad at him the day before our wedding, but *seriously*. The woman you're about to marry is having a fucking panic attack in the hotel room while you're out partying, and you can't even drop her a quick text? He kept saying he didn't want to message me and bother me. I didn't give a shit that he'd gone out or even stayed out so late, but I felt disregarded.

Our brief conversation about it while we got ready to leave for the catamaran, I concluded, was him simply defending his lack of respect or care for me.

Belief: I'm not as important to him as partying with his friends. He forgot about me.

Action: Be understanding, he doesn't get to see his friends often since they live far away.

Challenge: You are important. Even if he is with his friends, it would have taken less than 30 seconds to send you a text to let you know he was staying out and ask you how you're feeling. This was inconsiderate – a clear indication of behavior you are going to deal with in your marriage. You're panicking, he's partying, and you're the only one who cares.

***

We spent the day out on the catamaran with about twenty friends, dancing and downing a few watered-down rum punches. Seven of the guys, who'd all been out partying the night before, threw up over the side of the boat, and I joked that they were acting like they were still in their twenties when most of them were thirty- (or even forty-) something. We followed up with dinner and more drinks, accompanied by all 65 of our guests.

—

John and I went back to the hotel shortly before midnight. We both needed a good sleep after the colossal shitshow of the night before – and we were getting married tomorrow!

***

Friday morning. We woke up around 8:00 AM, exchanged our bride and groom gifts, and met everyone a couple hours later for breakfast at the restaurant by the beach. I gave our waiter some pesos in exchange for some bottles of champagne for me and my girls while we got ready for the ceremony, which he was happy to accept. I smuggled a couple back to the room in my large cross-body bag, and a couple of my bridesmaids did the same. I'm not much of a champagne drinker, but hey – it was my fucking wedding day!

After breakfast, we all went to the pool together for a couple hours, since I didn't need to start my preparations until about 2:00 PM. I'm just not very high maintenance, so I'd slated about two hours to get ready for the main event at 5:00 PM. I had my bridesmaids meet me in my room at 2:30. We all had a couple drinks and helped each other with our dresses, hair, and makeup, laughing, taking photos, and having fun the whole time. At 4:45, the golf carts arrived to shuttle us, one by one, to the ruins.

Holy shit, I thought. *I'm getting married!*

I'd planned out every detail of our wedding meticulously. The music, the attire, the bouquets, the lack of boutonnieres, the food, and drinks. Seeing it all come together was almost more exciting than the marriage I was entering into. As I walked down the aisle with my pseudo-dad, Sam, John teared up a bit – the second, and last, time he'd do so in front of me.

It's funny, really. I came to realize that those tears were, most likely, out of sadness over losing his player lifestyle. After all, it'd now be against the will of God, not just frowned upon. I'm not sure how that asshole ever kept a clean conscience being inside a church or claiming to be a Christian.

We'd written our own vows – once again, that was something *I* wanted. Mine were heartfelt and authentic. John's were, well, at least *true*. He tried to create a bit of comedy, but I didn't find them funny in the slightest.

"I will tune you out 90% of the time," he said, "but I would be lost without the sound of your voice. Yours is the only voice I want to hear until God takes me away."

Yeah? Well, God *would* end up taking me away from him, less than two years later. And he definitely tuned me out – not just my voice, my entire existence. This man did not want to be married. He just wanted the look of the wedded lifestyle, the pretty blonde wife with a successful career, and money. That's it.

How did I figure this out, you might ask? It was only three months until the mask started peeling off, and John's true narcissistic nature was revealed.

The Fuckery that is...

Photoshop.

"True love cannot be found where it doesn't truly exist. Nor can it be hidden where it truly does." – Francois de La Rouchefacould

The first couple months of our marriage were, much like my childhood move to South Carolina, a dream come true. We were going out on dates, enjoying each other's company, and falling into married life pretty comfortably.

My birthday weekend was coming up in late March, and I was a little bummed that he was going to miss it. He and his buddies took an annual "guys' weekend" to the Final Four basketball playoffs, which seems to always fall on my birthday. But I knew that already, and I'd accepted it for what it was. Besides, I was already planning a girls' trip to NYC with two of my friends to celebrate.

While my girlfriends and I were trekking all over Manhattan, I found myself feeling a little sad that my mother hadn't reached out. I decided to check in on Facebook, and saw photos posted of my mom and sister together. I didn't realize that they were from a few months prior, but in that moment, I thought they were together on a beach vacation. Man, what a fucked-up feeling. Mom would take trips to the beach with my sister, riding horses side by side, but couldn't spare five minutes to call and say happy birthday to me? True, I hadn't heard from Mom since before my wedding, which she didn't attend; but it was still gutting.

All I'd ever wanted was her love, support, and acceptance. Instead, I got nothing.

***

I decided it was time to cut that tie completely. Why was I continuing to let my mom drain me of happiness? So, I blocked her number, and started mourning the loss. She'd been toxic more often than not for my entire life; but she was still my mom, and the thought of leaving her behind forever hurt like a bitch.

John was a complete dick to me while I was grieving. One day, when we were driving to a football game, I told him how I was feeling. His response?

"I knew you shouldn't have come with me today. Do you really think I need to hear this right before I go play football?"

What? What in the actual, ever-loving fuck? It's co-ed, intramural, recreational, flag football, not the fucking Super Bowl! Asshole. I cried for a bit, then bottled up my emotions and carried on with the day.

Now, anyone can probably tell you (including me, in retrospect), that already feeling like this, along with other signs I was seeing, were pointing in the direction of "you fucked up when you married this man, Ty". But I'll spare you the ridiculous details of the countless acts of inconsideration, and other forms of bullshit, I was subjected to over the next few months. Let's just get right down to the juicy shit.

John's cousin's 40th birthday was in August, and they'd planned a guys' trip to Toronto for a weekend. His brother flew into Detroit to meet him, while his cousin headed straight to their destination. They took off on a Friday morning, and I wouldn't see him again until late Sunday night.

"Have a good time!" was about all I said as they started to drive the four hours to another damn country.

***

Fortunately, I'd invited a few of my girlfriends to come over that night for a sleepover. We had a couple drinks, put on our silly little onesies, and decided to walk to the nearby bar. We had a blast, laughing and drinking until the place closed. None of us cared if people thought we were nuts, sitting there wearing our unicorn, dinosaur, and duck adult-sized pajamas.

It was after 2 AM when we got home. I called John to check in and tell him about our night. We chatted for a few minutes, exchanging stories about our evenings – and then he hung up on me. I called back, thinking it was probably a mistake. He answered and hung up again.

"What happened?" I asked when I finally got him to talk to me.

"You know what you just said," he snapped.

"What?"

"You said the 'n' word."

"What are you talking about?!"

John didn't listen, just ended the call for a third time. Not only was this immature, but it was also *major* gaslighting. In what world would I have called any person of color, let alone the man I married, a derogatory name like that? I loved John, and I would *never* use that word to refer to him. The whole situation was just bizarre.

As I learned later that weekend, John had an agenda. He needed a reason to be mad at me and took it upon himself to create one.

***

I spent the next day in a state of severe depression. I hated being accused of something so horrific, when I knew I hadn't done anything to intentionally hurt him. I even spent two fucking hours on the phone with a suicide hotline. From losing my mom, to my husband treating me like I meant nothing to him, to work spiraling downward – and now this accusation? I needed someone to talk me off the metaphorical ledge.

Sunday evening, John returned home. He made me apologize for "what I said", which I did, despite knowing, to this day, that whatever I said was not what he thought he heard. We agreed to disagree.

Meanwhile, Facebook was surely listening to me when I was talking about him going out clubbing in Toronto, because I started getting served up adverts for venues there. I ignored the first couple – I mean, I work in social media marketing, of course these were popping up in my feed. But then, I see an ad for Everleigh Toronto Nightclub. And the image?

John. His cousin. Three girls. Holding shots and bottles of liquor.

Eh, no big deal, right? It's not unusual to meet or talk to people of the opposite sex when you're out partying. I've done it myself. Totally harmless if you're trustworthy and have no ill intentions.

But wait for it…

John wasn't wearing his wedding ring.

BAC?

Belief: He took his ring off so he would look single to cheat on me.

Action: Furious and curious, send him an instant text and ask him about it. Be open to hearing him out: maybe this was not on purpose, maybe he lost his ring. Whatever he tells you, know that you have the right to challenge it, because you had agreed to wearing wedding rings in your marriage.

Challenge: This guy has shown you time and time again that he is a self-centered person. He's lied to you almost constantly, and always has his own agenda. You are not his priority. Do not believe anything he tells you. Get out of this now.

Ugh. I did text him, and his knee jerk lie was simply outright fucking laughable. Are you ready for this?

John: They photoshopped it off!

Me: And they didn't photoshop anyone else's rings off in any of the other 100+ photos in the album from that night? Just yours?

John: I don't know, I guess!

Me: And did they photoshop *in* that little line where your ring should be?

Riddle me that. He should have known better than to start with this lie. I'm a Photoshop expert by trade, and I know it would have taken at least thirty minutes for a job like this one.

In less than an hour, he arrived home, and we sat down to talk about it. John changed his story. I stayed as calm and rational as a pissed-off, flustered wife could be.

"Why weren't you wearing your wedding ring?"

"You know what must have happened," he said, "actually, I took it off when I washed my hands in the bathroom and forgot to put it back on."

"So, it was in your pocket?" I asked.

"Yeah. And as soon as I realized, I put it back on. The picture was taken during those fifteen minutes or so."

"So why did you say they photoshopped it off?"

"It was just the first thing I thought, since I know I had it on all night."

"So, when you woke up the next morning, where was your ring?" I asked him.

"I don't know, everything was really fuzzy."

"But you just said you had it on all night," I countered.

"Ty, I don't know! But I wore my ring all night!" John insisted.

"Except for this one picture, right? You see how this looks don't you?"

"Yeah, but it's a coincidence," he said, with the look of a liar all over his face. "The picture must have been taken during those 10 minutes I didn't have it on after washing my hands. I put it on as soon as I realized!"

"You were mad at me for something you thought you heard me say, so you took it off on purpose. Is that what really happened? If so, just tell me. I'll understand."

"I *was* mad at you and had every right to take it off. I'd tell you if I did, but I *didn't*."

This was just circling around, going nowhere. We fought about this for a few days. The worst part wasn't that he was with other girls, or even took his ring off. It was the constant lying. He'd never give in, or admit he was the one in the wrong – narcissists never do.

I'd already started Googling what was happening between us; and every time I searched for these things, the one word that kept appearing was *narcissist*. *Holy shit*, I thought. *I'm married to a narcissist*. Then, *gaslighting*. Another realization – he gaslit me all the fucking time. If I challenged him on anything he did that was wrong, or inappropriate, or hurtful, it was always:

"You're too sensitive."

"You need therapy."

"You need medication."

"It was just a joke."

"You don't understand what you saw."

"You're overreacting."

This list could go on and on. Keep reading, and you'll see just how bad the gaslighting got the following summer, in a completely unedited letter from John that I received after I caught him in perhaps the biggest lie of them all.

That night he accused me of calling him the "n" word was pure gaslighting. He tried to alter my reality, to make me question what I *knew* was accurate. In turn, this gave him, in his mind, the *right* to take his ring off.

***

A couple years later, I made a TikTok about John's Photoshop lie, which ended up going viral. I even had Yahoo!, Google, and the *Daily Mail* covering it, in that highly exaggerated way the media usually does. The situation was still so comical to me – and, apparently, millions of others thought it was hilarious, too. With the hashtag #theliarwire, I proceeded to turn all his ridiculous lies into a smash-hit TikTok video series. So, thanks, John. I make money with every view of my content on TikTok, and I donate every last dollar I receive to help others in need.

The Fuckery that is...

Stealing.

"The most important human endeavor is striving for morality in our actions. Our inner balance and even our very existence depend on it. Only morality in our actions can give beauty and dignity to our lives." – Albert Einstein

Now, it was September. John had been offered a job transfer to Dallas, Texas. Deep down, I was hoping maybe this move would put us back on track, even though it was going to mean surrendering my comfort zone, my friends, my business I'd built in Detroit. I always put my marriage – and him – first.

His company, a huge international one that dealt in insurance, was going to pay full relocation. Nothing would be paid for out of our pocket, not a single flight, hotel, meal, or car hire, while we were searching for a new home.

***

After a weekend together in Dallas looking at houses, we were walking through Dallas Love Field Airport. John turned to me and said with excitement, "Hey, you know what we could do? We could submit an expense for breaking our lease and get reimbursed an extra $6,000!"

We weren't breaking our lease back in Michigan. In fact, Henry and Cindy were cool with our relocation, and had even decided to put the property on the market instead of renting it out again. They were letting us out penalty-free, even though the lease break fees would have been just one month's worth of rent.

"Why would we do that?" I asked.

"Because the company will pay for us to break the lease, up to three months of rent," John explained.

"That would only be if we actually were breaking our lease and having to pay the three months' rent penalty. That's why it's called a reimbursement."

"But we could so easily get an extra $6,000 if we did."

"John, that's just wrong. I'm not interested in sabotaging my karma while I'm about to try and get my company up and running in a whole new city."

"Okay, well, it's something to think about." He continued to try and get me on board with this crime.

"No. I'm not okay with it. If you do that, you better do it without telling me. I'm against it. But if you do, you better buy me something nice!" I joked to lighten the mood a little.

Nothing else was mentioned about the rent reimbursements, so I didn't worry too much after that.

***

About three weeks later, early one morning, I was outside with Bula.

"Hey, do you have a blank check I can borrow?" John asked, coming out to join us.

"Umm, sure. Yeah. What's it for?"

"I have to create an account for the relocation reimbursements, and I'm all out of checks."

I didn't think too much of this request, because his bank was based in Texas with no locations in Michigan. For John to be out of checks didn't seem unrealistic at all.

I tore off one of my blank company checks and handed it to him.

"Thanks!" He said.

***

Two days later, I asked John when I should start expecting the reimbursements in my bank account, since he'd used my check routing and account number.

"Oh, I changed the numbers, so I'll get the payments directly."

This was starting to sound weird. He'd already commented about one of my flight expenses getting deposited into his account on his regular payday. Something was definitely off.

"So, you used my check to do what, then?" I asked.

"They just needed a check image to upload, that's all."
"But you changed the numbers? How? To what, your routing and account number?"

"Yeah."

"Then why did they need an image at all, if you could just do that?"

"I don't know, I'm just getting reimbursed on payday now."

I knew this was a lie. I asked John to show me where he had uploaded my blank check. He opened his work phone, scrambled around for a few seconds, and then stuttered: "I don't have it. I don't know where it is."

"John, you didn't use my check for a relocation reimbursement account, did you?"

"Yes, I told you!"

I waited a couple days to further investigate this huge fucking load of bullshit he was telling me. After catching him in so many lies, John had agreed to let me check his phone any time I asked to. So, I did a little digging, and what did I find in his "Deleted Photos" album? A photo of my check, filled out to Cindy, for $5,700. The equivalent of three months' rent.

He did it, against my wishes and against my judgment. And he used my *company check*. Holy shit, this was *illegal!* I was fucking furious. My goal was to get him to admit he'd done it without having to tell him I knew. Of course, that didn't work.

***

The next few days were filled with tons of arguments and threats of divorce (from him, not me). I did my best to remain calm, asking him to please try and communicate in a healthier manner. For fear that if he were caught, it would come back on me, given that he had stolen nearly $6,000 using my bank account check, I recorded conversations where he admitted to doing it against my will. I had no intention of ever using it other than to defend myself if I were ever brought in for questioning.

Then I received an email from him, a forwarded message that he had simply typed above it:

I had the lease break rejected.

I noticed the only three words capitalized in the body of the email he'd forwarded were Lease, Break, and Rejected. Having a decent amount of programming knowledge, I thought perhaps it was a template that inserted words, as written, into a particular field.

My gut was telling me otherwise; but I wanted to believe John, and it *was* possible that those words were auto populated from an online form where he changed the status of the reimbursement. I had a BAC.

Belief: He said he had it reversed, so just accept it for what it is and move on.

Action: Since you're about to embark upon a whole new life together in a new state, let this go.

Challenge: This guy just literally told you he wanted to divorce you because you caught him in a lie, and stealing using *your* bank account. And you are fucking nuts if you think you're going to move across the damn country with him and things are going to get better. Fucking *nuts*. Do not go. Stay where you are supported by people who truly love you.

***

I'd find out two years later, after the divorce, that he never had the scam check for the relocation reimbursement rejected. Someone anonymously tipped off internal investigators, they questioned me, and I told the entire truth. John got fired in 2021.

Karma is a bitch.

The Fuckery that is...

A Fresh Start.

"No man, for any considerable period, can wear one face to himself, and another to the multitude, without finally getting bewildered as to which may be the true." – *Nathaniel Hawthorne,* **The Scarlet Letter** *(1850)*

A month or so after the check incident, we moved to Dallas. I didn't know anyone there; so, while John – every weekend night, it seemed – went out with his buddies, I'd stay home, mostly crafting and painting.

The situation didn't improve with time; and, come December, I'd had enough. I logged into Facebook to look up some local events, finding that Maverick, the bar down the street, was having an "Ugly Christmas Sweater" party. What better place to chill out, surrounded by others who just wanted to be comfortably silly for a few hours?

I fished out the only theme-fitting item of clothing I owned, ordered an Uber, and went to have a good time without that bastard.

That night, I gained several new friends – thanks, in part, to my sweater's declaration of *You used to call me on my elf phone*, a reference to that infinitely meme-able Drake track, "Hotline Bling" – as well as a staple local joint. John eventually agreed to start coming to the Maverick with me, and we got friendly with almost all the regulars. It was a comfortable little spot to hit once every week or two, kind of like our own version of Cheers!

***

John and I might have *looked* like a great couple; but, in reality, I'd become little more than a roommate. Any time we'd get into an argument, he'd toss his ring aside and leave for the day without wearing it. He slept on the couch. We rarely had sex. When I'd implore him to come to bed, he'd say, "Do you really think I want to sleep with someone who's *begging* me?" If I didn't ask, we didn't have sex. If I *did* ask, we didn't have sex. It was, you might say, the ultimate fucking catch-22.

The vacation to Mexico we'd planned for my 40th birthday was his new favorite ammunition. I'd paid for the trip (for both of us, as usual) two months in advance; and, when we'd get into these blowout fights, John would threaten to divorce me. Of course, I'd get anxious about spending my 40th birthday without him – I didn't want to lose him, or have to cancel the flights, or explain what had happened to everyone who'd planned to join us – and so I didn't tear him a new one and call him out on his manipulation. At the time, I wanted nothing more than for him to straighten up and gain some damn marriage maturity. You know, for him to actually act like he *wanted* to be my husband.

***

The nine of us – me, John, and some of our friends and family – spent an amazing five days in Mexico. Every day was filled with fun (sadly, not the sexy kind), with poolside activities like dance contests and games, volleyball, and excursions in the surrounding area.

That didn't, unfortunately, include my actual birthday.

I was standing outside the building where our room was located when a young guy walked up to me.

"Here. This is for your dude," he said, handing me a little bag with some white shit in it.

"Huh? What is this?"

"Your dude asked for this at the pool earlier today."

"You mean my husband?"

"Yeah. You're with the black guy, right?"

"Yeah… but he'd never ask for this. What the fuck?"

The guy looked just as confused as I felt as I handed the bag back to him and he walked away. I went up to our room, where John was still getting ready. He always took forever to get ready, mostly because he'd sit on the fucking toilet for an hour, playing some stupid game on his phone. We'd fight about it pretty often; and I once asked to see his weekly screen time, making a bet it was more than 9 hours a day. I was right.

I also bet you can guess what John was *really* doing on those supposed bathroom breaks.

Anyway, John was standing next to the bed, getting dressed.

"Hey, did you ask a guy at the pool today for drugs?" I said casually.

"Uh, um, no. Why?"

"Because some kid just tried to hand me a bag of, I don't know, maybe cocaine? It was white."

"Nope, not me."

Such a professional liar.

"Well, he certainly knew who you were," I went on. "And I'm pretty sure you and I are the only interracial couple at the pool, or even at this resort... Look, John – if you did ask for it, that's okay with me. Just let me know, that way I can take it easy and keep an eye on you. I mean, we *are* in Mexico!"

I was honest. It *was* fine with me if he'd bought some drugs. We were on vacation, who cares? It really wouldn't have been such a huge deal; other than the fact this was my 40th birthday and it would suck monumentally to have to babysit him instead of being able to let loose and celebrate this milestone.

John insisted he had no idea why this guy would have thought he asked for drugs. On that note, we proceeded out to dinner, the casino, the dance club, and the all-inclusive, 24/7 buffet. The night was topped off with a virtual bloodbath of a fight in the buffet line around 2:30 AM, the story of which was simply too good to leave out of this book.

Four of us – me, John, his buddy Jay, and Kelly (my pseudo sister) – were sitting at a table in the cafeteria, drunk as fuck. We heard people arguing, followed by crashes galore. They'd started throwing ceramic buffet plates at each other.

John and Jay, both over six-foot-three and 250 pounds each, rushed over to intercede. As they were trying to separate the two guys, one of whom was in a wheelchair, I saw a girl there, also yelling and looking like she was about to throw down. I staggered over and got in front of her.

"You don't wanna be involved in this, be a lady!" I slurred.

For a split second, she stopped, appearing to agree with me. Then she grabbed a plate and tossed it over my shoulder.

I went back to the table, slipping and sliding through puddles of blood that had formed on the floor, and sat down to watch the rest of the show.

Why the hell did these three decide that playing frisbee with the resort's crockery was the best way to resolve their argument? I have no fucking clue; but we did find out what started it when the security officers questioned us. The guy in the wheelchair was reaching for some pizza on the little heated turntable, when the other man came up behind him, grabbed his wheelchair handles, and pushed him out the way so *he* could get himself a slice of pizza! Even typing that out, I can't help but chuckle a little (in a "that's *so* fucked up" kind of way).

Welcome to 40, Ty! At least the first big fight didn't involve you.

———

The Fuckery that is...

Public Speaking.

"The one thing you are deathly afraid of is how someone else spends their life. Think about that." – Ty Paige

Summer was approaching, and I was due to give a presentation at a national marketing conference. I'd agreed to go, with more than a bit of reluctance – but it was way past time to overcome my fear of public speaking!

I flew out to Kansas City on a Tuesday afternoon. My speech was at 8:30 AM the following day. I didn't even have to tell John how nervous I was, with the endless hours of writing and practicing and the frantic, last-minute preparations he'd witnessed. All I'd asked was that he call me in the morning for one final pep talk. You know, the whole "You got this, babe!" shebang.

I woke up at 4:00 AM, anxiety chewing at my stomach. I'd wanted to spend a couple hours reciting my speech to make sure I had everything down, but this was way too early. I tossed and turned, telling myself I couldn't afford to be tired out for such an important occasion.

It was a failed effort.

I got up and started practicing. The morning hours slipped away, my head swimming, my pulse pounding. 7:00... 7:30... I still hadn't heard from John. I sent him a text, no reply. I called, no answer. 8:00... 8:15... and it was time for me to go on stage.

Somehow, I pushed aside my fears that something bad had happened to him. I powered through my 45-minute speech on Creative Social Strategies, shaking uncontrollably at first, then easing into it like a pro. In fact, my final rating was 4.7/5 – one of the highest of all 80 speakers at the entire event.

***

9:30 AM. Feeling hugely accomplished, but still worried that I hadn't heard from John, I went outside the venue to check my phone. Nothing.

I called him again. This time, he answered.

You already know, at this point, that I was about to be fed a shitload of lies. They went in this order:

"I took Benadryl after having a few drinks and it completely knocked me out."

"I didn't even wake up in time for work! I feel so guilty!"

"I went to bed at midnight. I don't know why I slept so late."

I knew he'd been out with his cousin, who was in town for a couple days; but that in no way excused the shit he'd pulled. I asked him if he thought I was in the right to feel hurt by his lack of support, and he – shockingly – agreed.

My evening flight felt like an eternity away. I couldn't sit there and wait, potentially giving John the chance to cover up the truth. So, I switched to an earlier one, without telling him, and went straight home.

***

I walked in hours before he was expecting me.

The place was *trashed*. John's cousin, perched on the couch, came right on out with how they'd partied all night – clearly, they hadn't yet discussed the lie they were going to tell me. He also mentioned they'd brought some people back to our house from the Maverick.

Oh, really? Who could be more important to John than his *wife*, who'd just faced her biggest fear in life without his support?

The next time we went to the Maverick, I found out: a couple of guys I didn't know, and a girl named Hattie, who identified as lesbian. I approached her, because I am not the type of girl who just lets her husband bring random women back to the house when she's out of town.

Our conversation was pretty straightforward; and, after we talked, I felt I had a better idea of what happened that night – something I'd never get from John's dishonest mouth. At least Hattie seemed to be genuine with me and understanding about how upset and pissed-off I was.

***

After that whole fucked-up episode, I couldn't settle down. I felt betrayed and used – and trapped.

In that moment, I had the kind of BAC that kicked my ass.

Belief: You made this commitment. You have to try your best to honor it. Maybe, one day, he will change.

Action: Just keep plugging along and enjoy the good times you have together. Show him you're committed and keep praying for everything to work out.

Challenge: You married this guy one day after he showed you who he really was. You keep staying. Every time he fucks up and you don't leave, you're showing him that he can do whatever he wants and get it away with it. Girl, *get the fuck out!*

The Fuckery that is...

A Girls' Trip.

"I need my friends like I need my breath. I just can't live without them." – Ty Paige

A month later, I was discussing going on a girl's trip – to somewhere tropical, of course! – with a couple of my new Dallas-area girlfriends. John took his "guys' trips" at least two or three times a year, so I knew he wouldn't have a problem with it.

I pride myself on being the "travel agent" of my friends and family, and I immediately began searching for the best deals on cool places. I found a super-cheap flight to Saint Maarten in the Caribbean; then, after a bit of digging, *boom* – a two-room apartment villa at a resort right by Maho Beach! The total cost came to about $400 per person for five days, including airfares and accommodation.

I invited two of my girlfriends from back home to join and proceeded to get *super* stoked about the six of us jetting off to an island paradise that summer!

***

One weekend after the girls and I booked our trip, John and I were supposed to drive to his hometown for his friend's crawfish broil. The morning we were set to go, he threw his stuff into a bag and just fucking *left*. Without me!

I pulled him into the bedroom, crying, asking what the hell he thought he was doing.

"I don't want to see your face this weekend!" He snapped.

I started sobbing so hard I threw up. John grabbed his bag and stomped off, slamming the garage door behind him as he left the house, and me, sitting on the bathroom floor hugging the toilet.

I did receive a drunken phone call around 3:00 AM from him and his cousin, and we talked for a few minutes. After I filed for divorce, I'd find out that, surprise, surprise, he cheated on me that night with a girl he knew back home.

When John and I weren't fighting, we were mostly on autopilot. He played his stupid game and sat on the toilet, while I worked my ass off, trying to get more business for my struggling marketing agency. He went off and did his thing with his buddies or co-workers, I'd meet up with my girlfriends for happy hour once a week at a new bar called Chill; and, *occasionally*, we'd go out together to the Maverick or to his niece's or nephew's sports games.

***

The Dallas girls and I left for Saint Maarten on a Wednesday, with an overnight stop in Fort Lauderdale to meet up with the others before flying direct to the island. It was so refreshing to be amongst good friends, just letting loose, having fun, and not worrying over when John would finally act like he gave a shit about me.

The first night, we all went out dancing and met a group of ladies who were also on a girls' trip. We were pretty beat from the day's travelling (and misplacing passports and bits of luggage), but damn if we didn't find the energy to share a few more drinks and soak up the party spirit!

I'd missed a call from John while we were out. He'd left me a voicemail saying he really needed me – like, in the "hey, something terrible happened and I need you to be there for me" kind of way – and, of course, me with my empath nature was worried like crazy. John hadn't left any other details, so I called him back as soon as I could. He didn't answer.

It was only 11:30 PM back home. What could be keeping him unless it really *was* something awful? I sent John a text, telling him to call me any time; I'd keep my phone on for him.

No reply.

Come morning, I still hadn't heard anything. I tried calling and texting again, nothing.

My phone finally lit up with John's number around noon. He said he'd found out his daughter's maternal grandmother was ill – nothing serious, thankfully – and just really needed someone to talk to, but he was fine now. My gut was telling me something was definitely not right. Even when the girls tried to reassure me, or said I was just being dramatic or paranoid, I couldn't shake the feeling.

I sat there on our ocean-view terrace, with Shelly, Maggie, and a couple of the others, trying not to think too much about the "shituation". That's when Sue, who was still inside and butt-naked, came singing and dancing over to the glass door wall and pressed her bare tits up against it. As we all burst into hysterical laughter, I felt all my worries being swept away.

***

The rest of our vacation was nothing short of amazing. Day drinks by the beach, where the airplanes would pass so low, we could almost touch them; dancing and dinners; random trips in pickup trucks. Drunken, 4:00 AM luggage cart rides that once ended with a mild concussion (yup, Sue again). Pool volleyball. Swimming off the docks by the bay. We were having the time of our lives, and we never wanted Monday to come.

Alas, it did. One of my Dallas girlfriends and I shared an Uber from the airport since we lived so close to each other. That's right – my dear hubby wouldn't even pick me up after not seeing me for almost six days. I'd always driven *him* back and forth when he went out of town for his guys' weekends! Ugh. It makes me sick to think about how I went so far above and beyond for this man who was more concerned with making up lies so he could fuck other women behind my back.

When I walked in the door, John was asleep on the couch. I said hi and went over to him; but he acted disturbed by my presence, so I just went on unpacking and giving Bula lots of love. I went to take her outside and noticed the back porch light was on.

I never turned that light on. I hated doing it – the glow attracted way too many bugs. And John never went outside, like, ever…

"Hey babe, why is the light on?" I asked as I came back in.

"I was out there with Bula earlier and turned it on."

"Oh. But it was light out, then."

"I really don't know, Ty," he huffed. "Leave me alone."

I got those "leave me alone" vibes a lot from John, these days. It'd become fairly normal for me to feel completely disregarded. Even though I'd been gone for almost a week, he didn't even care to get up and give me a hug.

I went to bed alone, as usual.

***

The next morning, I did my normal ritual: wake up, make some coffee, sit out on the back porch with Bula. I'd put an old coffee can there for an ashtray, but I'd emptied it when I left for my trip. Why, then, were there eight or nine cigarette butts in it?

I intercepted John right before he left for work.

"Hey, there's a bunch of cigarette butts outside. Whose are they?"

"I don't know, probably the lawn guys'."

"They don't smoke," I pointed out. "I work from home, and I see them every week."

"Well, probably your friends', when they were here last."

"No, I cleaned it out before I left. These ones are all new."

"I don't know how they got there then, Ty. Why are you interrogating me?"

"Because I know someone was here! Just tell me who. It's no big deal. Why won't you tell me?"

"Ty, NO ONE WAS HERE!"

Even as John raised his voice at me, I kept going. I insisted I didn't care if someone had been there, but just to tell me. He refused to admit it, though, heading out to work still denying everything.

I spent the entire day unsettled; and, when John got home, I asked him again. He left the living room, barely acknowledging that I'd said anything.

He did, eventually, give me a variety of bullshit responses:

"You know I wouldn't have anyone here while you're out of town."

"You're crazy if you think I would have anyone over here."

"You know I'm not the type of person to have parties here."

"I wouldn't have anyone over here, because I know you wouldn't like that."

Sure, John. Thanks *so* much for the clarification. It might have worked if I didn't know deep down it was all total fucking bullshit.

The Fuckery that is...

The Truth.

"Character is doing the right thing when nobody's looking. There are too many people who think that the only thing that's right is to get by, and the only thing that's wrong is to get caught." – J. C. Watts

Since John had made it screamingly obvious he didn't want to be around me, I decided to go meet my girlfriends for a beer at the Maverick. I hadn't even been home 24 hours, but I wasn't going to sit at home with this asshole making me feel like I was crazy!

The four of us sat around a table outside for about an hour. I had one beer, which was all I'd really planned on having. I told them about the bullshit going on at the home front, and they all agreed something seemed fishy. What I didn't know was that the guy sitting at the table next to us had overheard the whole conversation.

Keep in mind, this little bar is a local hangout. Everyone knows everyone, and there was always some drama to steer clear of.

***

I got home at 9:00 PM and changed for bed. As I was brushing my teeth in the bathroom, I heard my phone ding. It was Facebook Messenger. I finished up and retrieved my phone from where I'd tossed it on the bed.

Jimmy Andrew would like to send you a message.

I tapped on the notification.

Hey heard you found cigarettes at your house they are from my ex that went there I was gonna tell you tonight cause I thought it was wrong in general

It took a couple minutes for this to sink in. I stalked the guy's Facebook profile and quickly realized who he was. Jimmy was a regular at the Mav, well-known for being a druggie. He was also notorious for his on again, off again relationship with a girl named Lori, another regular with similar vices. I'd never hung out with them, but I knew *of* them.

My hands were shaking, and my heart was fucking pounding out of my chest. I replied:

Who is your ex?

You can now message and call each other appeared on the screen.

Thanks, Facebook. You're about to ruin my life.

Lori.

Jimmy dropped the bomb.

Are you serious?

Yeah. Not happy about it either.
How do you know for sure? How? What night was that?

With every stupid little animated bubble that indicated he was typing, my chest got tighter and tighter. I was right. I fucking knew it. I was right.

Jimmy: Watched them leave together then she told me she went there to your house and I think Thursday I would have to look

Me: Do you have proof? Like a text?

Jimmy: Hold on

Me: I'm shaking right now. She smokes Camel menthol?

Jimmy: No that's the other girl

Oh. My. God. There was another girl involved. Fuck.

What other girl? I asked him.

He sent several screenshots of a text thread between him and Lori. It even included a photo of my house. Jimmy continued to tell me how she'd cheated on him before, and he believed something happened with her and John. Lori had been at my house until almost 6:00 AM, along with none other than Hattie, the girl John had invited over when I was at the conference. I'd learn later than Hattie was John's coke supply, and more likely a bisexual friend with benefits than his strictly lesbian friend.

I took some time to calm down before I went to the living room, where John was half-asleep on the couch. He always just lay there like this sad, lifeless log, with his dad belly making a permanent dent on the couch cushion. Everything that originally attracted me to this guy was long gone, and how or why I'd *ever* beg him to sleep with me boggles my mind, now.

I stood there, glaring at him, adrenaline racing in my veins, blood thundering through my heart. For a few seconds, I couldn't say anything. He'd always done such a good job of manipulating me and altering my perception of reality, I had to muster up the courage to state the facts without letting him get away with his usual gaslighting.

"Who is Lori?" I demanded.

"Who? What?"

"You are *busted*."

With literally no emotion, no reaction, he rolled off the couch, got up, and walked to the bedroom. I didn't follow him. I didn't even cry. I just stayed there, in shock, for what felt like an hour.

***

The next morning, I ignored John as he got ready and left for work. I spent hours on the phone with my friends, trying to figure out what to do. I didn't have any more details, aside from what Jimmy had said, about the night John had Lori and Hattie over, but I felt deep down that he'd been unfaithful.

Right around lunchtime, my phone buzzed again. It was John.

"So, I guess we should talk?" he said.

Jesus, John. For real? You can't sit down and have a mature, in-person conversation, so you call me from work? Fine.

We talked. He told me that he was at the Maverick with Hattie, and Lori had gotten upset and started to walk home. She'd been drinking a lot, so Hattie suggested they go pick her up and take her home. They dropped her off – then she drove over to our house, where John and Hattie were already hanging out. He said that was it, they just hung out, nothing happened.

"Why didn't you just tell me?" I said. "You *know* I wouldn't have cared if you had just told me. Like, the very next day."

"I knew you'd assume something happened and get upset."

"Okay, I see why you might think that, but can I get a little credit? I tell you about everything I do because I don't have anything to hide. Even if it includes a guy."

"We just decided that it'd be best not to tell you about it. We all agreed."

"Oh, wow, John! So, you're having women over, partying until the sun comes up, while I'm out of town, making pacts to keep secrets from me? I'm just... I'm done. *I'm leaving.*"

That call went on for about twenty minutes, and, in my state of heavy-hearted exhaustion, I couldn't remember all of it. I know he admitted to having the girls over, and to lying, and he didn't oppose my decision.

So, I left.

***

I packed a small suitcase and went to Shelly's, where I planned to stay until I figured out what to do. My marketing agency, which had once earned over $300K annually in revenue, had dwindled down to about $80K since I'd moved to Dallas. This city wasn't right for me, a hard-working entrepreneur who didn't have a silver spoon in her mouth.

Shelly and I sat on her balcony, beers in hand. I swear, every other sentence out of my mouth was:

"What do I do?"

The last BAC I had kept replaying in my mind. I married this guy knowing, in my gut, that he was not going to treat me the way I wanted to be treated. I wasn't the type of wife to pull the wool over my eyes when things went bad or wrong. He knew that and married me anyway. We both stood at that altar knowing he couldn't be the man I needed, and I wasn't the woman he wanted.

He needed someone who would never challenge him the way I did.

***

A couple days later, I was sitting in the CVS Pharmacy parking lot and called John. I don't know why.

"I'm re-evaluating my entire life right now," he said.

"Why is that?"

"Because it's pretty bad when a crackhead has more clout than I do."

That's a real fucking valid point, John. In fact, that one sentence summed up the entire situation. It also gave me a sliver of hope: maybe he'd finally open his eyes and see what he was about to lose.

Two days after that conversation, I got a text from him. He told me he was sending me an email and asked me to read it carefully several times with an open mind.

I should have guessed how this was going to go. No way in hell was this guy going to change. But I did what he asked.

The Fuckery that is...

Gaslighting.

"Giving someone a second chance is like giving them an extra bullet for their gun, because they missed you the first time." – Unknown

Before you read the email John sent me, note the following:

1. I paid for our vacations, wedding, and honeymoon. I even lent him money any time he was short (which happened several times). We never combined finances. He didn't pay for my phone or car insurance; I paid him every single month for both (we were on shared plans). The utilities were always split. Some months I'd pay the power, and he'd pay the gas or streaming. I paid for way more, throughout our relationship, than he ever did.

2. Yes, I had a rough childhood – as you've read – but to throw it at me, to use it as ammunition when he was the one lying to me, is gaslighting.

3. Also gaslighting: keeping secrets, and being deceitful, because "I can't handle the truth" is such fucking bullshit.

The only example of this he could even give me was an incident where his swinger co-worker sent pictures of himself fingering his wife and three other girls at the same time. I told John I was not okay with him receiving those photos, which was my right as his wife. That's not a lifestyle I want to be part of, and as far as I knew (from what John had told me), John wasn't into that either. So yes, I had asked him to politely tell his perverted, aspiring-porn-star friend to not send that stuff anymore.

The only edit I have made to this email is changing names to protect the identities of those mentioned.

I have a lot to say about us. Just know that I am just being honest and coming from a place of love. This is going to be the most open and honest I have ever been so please read through it and don't just pick out sections to criticize.

I want to start with things that I hold back instead of bringing them up. I do this quite often and it is not healthy. Therefore, I won't be holding back anymore. The reason I hold back feelings and eat a lot myself is that I know your life has not been easy. You have had to endure things that I cannot understand. So when you do things that upset me, I tend to hold back and tell myself that it is not your fault and that you have just been dealt a rough hand in life.

One of the most recent things involves money. I have taken over your car insurance, phone, health insurance, our retirement plan (in which I increased my deductions as it is not just me anymore), life insurance and took over the electric bill. I understand you went through a rough patch and I was willing to do whatever I could to make sure we were ok. However, as soon as you started getting some payments in, you never offered to pick up the electric one month or even pay your portion of insurance or phone. You booked a vacation, went shopping and constantly order things on Amazon. Every time a new package shows up here, my frustration level doubles. You don't seem to mind that I am paying for all these things and have limited income. Even the Sue money that she loaned you. I paid your debt to her because I felt horrible about vacationing in Mexico while you still owed her money. I could not enjoy that trip until I made sure that she was repaid. This is who I am. I do not party on other people's money until that debt is repaid. This didn't seem to bother you. However, I swallowed it, paid it and made sure your party was a success.

Swallowing these emotions does have a side effect as I do get distant at times. This is why I need decompression time. I tell myself, "she has had a hard life and it's not her fault."

The next subject is something that you will disagree about but I am going to say it anyway. I have been conditioned to not tell you everything because of the way you handle some situations. I didn't wake up one day and figure that I was only going to tell you partial things. There are numerous times in the past in which I have given you the whole story and you do not handle it well. Due to the multiple times, I started holding back more and more.

Then we land on this week when I held back something that was perfectly innocent in fear of how you would react. The truth of the matter is, I have to often go back behind you and apologize and smooth things over. I do this because I love you and "you have had a hard life" so you don't really mean ill. This didn't start in Texas. It started in Michigan. Maybe your friends are too afraid to say this but I have pulled most of them aside and apologized for the way you have reacted or treated them on multiple occasions,

—

including Annie. I know more to that story but that is between you two to work out. Whether it's something you have done drunk or when you were in a pissed off mood. I have always talked to them and said, "You know how Ty feels about you. She considers you family. Do not take what she said to heart. You know how hard her life has been. She doesn't mean it."

Yes I did this behind your back but for your benefit. You can pretty much ask any of them. We have all had these conversations but all love you dearly. We do not say anything because it will not go over well and we know it.

As far as the other night, I did not do anything that we would not have done together. It was not a plan to come here afterwards. We just ended up being near the house after chasing down Lori in Hattie's truck. Our big secret pact wasn't about not telling you about us being here. It was about the content of our conversation. We got really drunk and everyone told some really personal shit, which has not came out in all this. The only reason not telling you about us being here came up was due to the reaction last time. You ripped Hattie enough for her to come find me at the bar and ask if everything was ok. I didn't want that happening again. You say you didn't but maybe you don't realize that you did. I am not making this up. I just didn't want you blowing things up for no reason. So I chose to lie to you. Not my proudest moment and it was a terrible decision. I am not arguing that. For that, I deserve everything that you are throwing my way because I violated your trust. I challenge you to think about this in a different way. Ask yourself why I feel like I need to hide things from you...

You don't have to worry about me hiding things from you as I plan on speaking my mind every day. It is not fair for me to hold things in until I blow up and it is not fair to you know hear the truth daily.

As far as my feelings, I love you and there is no doubt about it. I have never and will never cheat on you as you are everything I need. I am almost 40 and I have had my freedom and I will gladly do it all over again with you given the chance. You are right. I have approached this wrong. I have been closed off. I have been distant. However, it is not for the reasons you think. It is not because I want out or I look at other women wishing I was with them instead of you. I just hold back because I don't know what I am going to get by bringing things up with you. You will not like that statement as you think your reactions are always good. I am telling you that they are not.

Are you willing to accept my feelings on this matter? I am willing to be so straight forward that you are going to want me to shut up at times. I have no choice in the matter because, if we are going to be together forever, I will have a heart attack due to stress in the next 10 years. This is my change. This is who I need to be to be truly happy and a good husband. The only thing I need from you is to listen to what I am saying instead of disregarding it and proving your point by picking out partial truths from the past. I am imagining you reading this and having 15 different arguments ready to tell me how wrong I am. However, this is how you make me feel. These are my feelings and how I have been made to feel. If you disregard what I have written today then there is no hope. I need to make changes and I readily admit that I have not handled things correctly and that is why we are here today. Can you at least read this message one more time before responding with several reasons why I am wrong? Like I said, this is how I have been made to feel and I know you are not purposely doing this. I am in no way blaming you for where we are today. I have admitted that my handling of our relationship has been wrong am I am starting with this letter.

In the end, I love you and all your flaws. I love the way you make me feel and I love the way you look at me. I love waking up beside you and I want to do us forever. Changes are being made on my end and I hope that you read this with an open mind and find the changes I need to be happy as well. I know you have had a hard life and my only wish is to make it better.

Way to turn things around on me, John. I never claimed to be perfect. I definitely do have my flaws. But here we were, after *he had fucked up*, not me. He managed to find a way to make it all about him, his feelings, and how *I* needed to change. So not cool.

I read that email at least ten times before taking any further action. If he were smart, he wouldn't have asked me to read it over more than once, because the first time, I felt some empathy for him. By the tenth time, I was flat-out fucking mad. He had the audacity to make this about how *I* was in the wrong.

I stood there on Shelly's balcony and had a BAC.

Belief: He is open to change, take that for what it is. Did he cheat? Probably. But you will never know, and it is out of your control at this point.

Action: Go home and talk to him. Work this out, and see if he does, in fact, make changes.

Challenge: This entire letter is narcissistic and gaslighting. The parts where he gives any admission of wrongdoing are not genuine apologies, they are just his sad attempts to lessen the guilt he feels for getting caught, not for what he did. If you go back to him, this will be the ultimate proof to him that he can – and will – do whatever the fuck he wants, whenever the fuck he wants. After a couple arguments over things he does wrong, he will just expect you to sweep it under the rug just like you have for a year and a half.

My friends *are* my family; so, of course, John claiming that he'd had to apologize to them for things I'd said or done really upset me. I reached out to them to ask if his comments held any truth.

Five of my closest, most trusted friends all replied the exact same way. "What?" or "Huh?" followed by "Uh, no. He's never apologized for you, and you've never done anything." All but Sue, who jokingly texted:

IDK probably but that's what we do, we piss each other off sometimes haha!

John really didn't like when I told him what I'd done. Narcissists hate when you call them out on their bullshit. He kept right on

---

91

with his crap, saying, "They just don't want to tell you."

Excuse me? My friends and I have always been – and always will be – up front with each other. We've been brutally honest about anything and everything: our feelings and emotions, picking sports teams, what looks good or doesn't. (Yeah, I'm *that* person who'll tell my girlfriend if something doesn't suit her.) They'd never keep the truth from me.

***

In spite of all this, I went back to the house that weekend. John and I ended up talking, and we decided we'd give this one more shot. I really wanted to make it work so I agreed to be careful with how I reacted to things; and I told him I needed him to trust me and believe that he could be honest with me. The things that had happened up until this point were upsetting, yes – because it seemed as though he didn't want to be married. His actions, and behavior, were more aligned with those of a single guy. If I didn't see more maturity from him – and if he didn't stop fucking lying – I was out.

The Fuckery that is...

Fingers and Toes.

"Sometimes we hold onto something because we are afraid of what life would look like without it." – Ty Paige

A week later, we'd been invited to John's friend's house for a double-date pool party. We ate burgers, had some beers, and hung out all day. When we got home, though, things escalated. I was still dealing with a lot of emotions about his recent all-night party, the lies surrounding it, and, most of all, the intuition that John had cheated on me with Lori. So, I foolishly – and drunkenly – brought it up.

We fought hard. In typical John style, he tried to leave, to get away from the conversation; and I, being way too tipsy, was crying and begging him to stay. At one point, I grabbed his arm and tried to pull him back to me, which ended up with his head getting caught in the door. He'd later try to portray this as some sort of deliberate, abusive action, when all I wanted was for him to stay with me, hold me, and reassure me that nothing had happened between them.

***

I ended up leaving for the second time the next day. Shelly had started dating a guy named David and spent most of her time at his place, so she'd given me a key to her apartment. It was good for me, being alone. I got to really spend some time thinking about things. John, I concluded, was the one who'd put us in this monumental "shituation". I shouldn't be sitting here feeling guilty!

And so, I decided, in a moment of epic, mid-week "fuck it", to take David up on his offer to go stay with him and Shelly at his house.

**

My marriage was over. I knew it, deep down, and the thought devastated me. Luckily, I had Shelly and David to lean on for support. One day, when we were sitting by his pool, David asked me why I'd even consider staying with this douchebag who'd been so neglectful of me. He asked me to just start reciting all of the incidents out loud.

"Well, let's see. It started with Amanda. Then Nicole. Then Cristina. Then the whole Layla thing. Then there was the check bullshit, Toronto, the lie about the Mexican cocaine, the speaking engagement fuck-up, Lori and Hattie, leaving me alone that one weekend..."

I went on and on, naming girls and using other monikers to allude to each shitty event, every time he'd hurt me. David was counting on his fingers at first, then moved to his toes. After I'd said the twentieth occurrence out loud, he told me to stop. He looked at me and said, "I'm off my fingers and my toes... Do you need any more clarity? The guy is scum. You deserve better."

He was right – but I had committed to a marriage. I wasn't even sure if it was a last bit of love keeping me invested in John, or just my ego. Whatever it might be, I still couldn't bear the idea of leaving for good just yet.

The Fuckery that is...

Narcissism.

"Lies don't end relationships, the truth does." — *Shannon L. Alder*

Mid-September. John and I were out at the Maverick, and I was on crutches because I'd torn the ligaments in my ankle. He didn't know, but I wasn't really drinking that night. I'd gotten to the point where I was tired of his gaslighting me when we were drunk. I wanted to be sober, to keep a clear head so I'd know exactly what was happening.

We were walking across the street to the Waffle House when, out of nowhere, he got mad and started heading home – without me. He left me standing on the sidewalk by the restaurant, confused as fuck.

"What are you doing?" I yelled at his back. "What did I do?"

I hobbled back over to the Mav, where I was re-greeted by an older guy who we knew pretty well.

"What's wrong? What happened?" he asked me.

"I have no idea. He just left."

"You aren't drunk or anything. Is he?"

"I didn't think he was. He just said he was pissed off and walked away!"

I ordered an Uber and went straight home. When I arrived, I crutched through the door into the living room, finding John flopped on the couch, as usual.

"What did I do, John?" I repeated. "Why did you leave me?"

"If you don't know, I'm not going to tell you."

What. The. Fuck.

"I don't know, and I only had one beer tonight. You probably thought I had more, but I didn't."

"You know what you said."

"No, John, I do not. I didn't say anything. We were just crossing the street, and out of nowhere you said you were pissed at me."

"Like I said, Ty – I'm not going to satisfy you by telling you what you said if you don't remember."

I swear, this dude could write an instructional book on gaslighting. Just a week later, we went to a grand opening party hosted by one of his friends. I was still in my "fake-out drinking" phase, so I only had one glass of wine. He'd been sick the week prior and I guess hadn't eaten much junk. On the way out, I asked if I should grab him a couple of cupcakes for the road.

"You know I don't eat sweets!" he shouted at me.

My face still scrunches up in the most awkward, squishy expression of confusion when I think about that statement he made. You know why? Because the next day, he was standing in the kitchen eating ice cream.

I had to take this shot to call John out on his bullshit. How the hell could he deny this (I thought, believing I knew exactly what I was doing *facepalm*)? I looked at him and said, "I thought you didn't eat sweets?"

"Oh, are you judging me now because I have a sweet tooth?" he growled.

He used to tell me how his daughter's mother had bipolar disorder, but I always wondered if he might have had a touch of it himself. At the time, I wasn't sure what else could possibly make someone act like two completely different people from one day to the next.

***

The summer before, when I'd first discovered the concept of a narcissistic personality, I'd talked about it to a good friend of mine back in Detroit. He told me he never liked John from the start, that something was way off about him and his constant need to be liked by everyone. I hadn't noticed it before; but over the course of my marriage to John, it became more and more clear. This guy was *whoever* he needed to be in front of *whoever* he was with. The stories he'd tell sometimes didn't even make sense. I remember one fall day in 2018, the first year we were married, when I asked him to tell me three things he thought I was good at. I knew it was always a competition with John, that he'd use any excuse to one-up me.

Scratch that – John would one-up anyone if it meant he came out on top. One night, we were out with two of my good friends, James and Kelly, who'd just gotten married in Mexico. They were talking with another friend of theirs about how tan they got during their vacation, and John just *had* to butt in with, "I'm still the tannest of you both!" Well, of course you are, you idiot. You're Black. They're white.

The two guys just rolled their eyes at him.

The Fuckery that is...

Deleting Texts.

"At some point you just have to say, "fuck you, watch this", and walk away with a smile – and a nice ass." – Ty Paige

Fast forward another month. John had been offered a position that would relocate us to Phoenix, Arizona, and he'd accepted it. I was excited about yet another opportunity to start over somewhere new together, as a last-ditch effort to save our marriage. Our realtor was scheduled to host an open house viewing of our place on a Saturday afternoon, and it just so happened that two of John's friends were going to be in town that weekend.

Ethan and Jen (who'd been staying at John's, all that time ago, the first time he and I ever had sex) lived in Austin, Texas. When they arrived, we went out for drinks at the Maverick. After a fun-filled night of introducing them to local friends, getting a bit wasted, and laughing our asses off, we stumbled home. John had invited Hattie to come with us – something I privately took issue with, but I didn't bring it up with him. I was tired and overserved, and I didn't want to cause a scene when we had guests.

Surely John wouldn't dream of doing anything inappropriate while I was in the house?

***

I woke up early the next morning, around 7:00 AM. To my surprise, Hattie was *still* there.

I headed outside, trying not to let on that I was upset. She and John hadn't stopped partying; in fact, they were still mixing drinks when I showed up. We had some friendly banter, and Hattie finally left a couple hours later.

Ethan and Jen were still in bed, thank fuck, so I was able to help John to bed without any awkward questions. He was absolutely hammered. I tucked him in and told him to get a couple hours of sleep – the realtor was coming at noon.

While I was pinching the blankets around him, John's phone went off. It was in his pocket, so I grabbed it and plugged it in for him, setting it on the nightstand.

The text was from Hattie.

When I went back downstairs, Ethan and Jen were sitting in the living room. They started asking me about Hattie: who she was, why she'd come back to our place, why she'd spent so much time with John.

"She's one of John's drinking buddies," I told them. "I don't mind him having them over now and then; but yeah, it's weird they stayed up all night together."

I took Bula out and decided to check the footage from the front-door security camera footage. There was a block of time, from 5:00 AM until about 6:30 AM, where the camera was facing the ground. I studied the video right before and right after, saw that John had repositioned it when he and Hattie went to the porch. I caught a little of their conversation, too. He told her I was crazy. Likely story. That's what he called all of his exes, too.

***

Noon was fast approaching, and we had to get John out of bed before the realtor arrived. I thought the best thing to do was to make him a drink – a Crown Royal whiskey, of course. We pulled at him, shook him, even propped him up from underneath to get him into some sort of half-alert state. I eventually demanded he get up. It was *his* choice to party for 15 hours straight, and he had to face the consequences. No way in fucking hell was the realtor going to show our home with a passed-out drunk guy in the bed.

Ethan strolled in with the whiskey. John sat up, begrudgingly, and gulped it down before heading to the bathroom.

Please, dear God, do not *take your usual hour-and-a-half in there.*

The realtor showed up, and I greeted her briefly as we left the house – thankfully, with John in tow. As we sat in the back of the Uber driver's shiny new Lincoln Navigator, heading out to watch some college football at a nearby Michigan State bar, John even reached over and held my hand.

Something felt off, way off.

***

The bar was crowded with people, standing around the tables, perched up at the bar, and filling the outdoor picnic benches. All the big college games were playing on the television screens in every corner.

We managed to find one open table outside and all sat down together, John to my left. Very quietly, I asked him to show me the texts between him and Hattie. I said I was interested in understanding the dynamic of their friendship, especially since they'd spent all night together and he'd taken extreme measures to keep the camera from capturing whatever they were doing.

"John, show me the texts between you two. I know she was texting you this morning when you were going to bed."

"I will later."

"Why later? Just show me now."

He opened his phone and scrambled around for a minute.

"Oh, they're not here," he said, looking at me with an idiotic glare. "I don't know where they are."

Seriously, dude? You fucking *deleted* them. I was pissed, but I couldn't show it much, us being in public and all.

"You deleted them. I know you did," I said calmly. "Why? What were you texting about?"

He got angry – I mean, *really* fucking angry. I told him I'd ask Hattie for screenshots if he wasn't going to come clean, and he got up and stormed off.

We watched as John hailed an Uber to go home, dumbstruck, in disbelief that this, *this* was how I was treated after *he* had fucked up *yet again*. As his car pulled up at the corner, I looked at him and shook my head side to side in disappointment. John proceeded to give me the middle finger and mouth "fuck you" in my immediate direction. Ethan and Jen saw it, too.

***

I had to let the realtor know John was on his way back, but damn if I'd give her the real reason why. "Hey, so my drunk, asshole husband just told me to fuck off and is on his way home to go back to bed during the open house!" No way. How fucking embarrassing! So instead, I opted for, "Hey, John isn't feeling well. He's on his way back to take a lie down. Hopefully that won't disturb the open house too much. I'm so sorry!"

The three of us spent the next few hours walking around and sipping lattes and tea from a little café. We sat in the lounge chairs, talking about everything that John had put me through. Ethan and Jen hadn't had a clue. They told me they were disgusted with his behavior, that a married man shouldn't be acting the way John did. They had no intention of staying with us that night after what they'd seen and decided to pack up and leave.

I don't blame them. In fact, I don't believe they have even been in touch with John since that whole shitshow. The three of us, however, have been fortunate enough to stay friends.

***

John was still in bed when we returned, and the realtor had left. Ethan and Jen – and I – grabbed our stuff and got the hell out. I still had the spare key to Shelly's place, so I went there, determined to stay until John left for Phoenix the next day. I was supposed to be following him out on Monday night, so we could look for houses together, but I was so mad and confused I had no idea what to do.

As luck would have it, come Sunday night, I was in excruciating pain from a toothache and ended up having to have emergency dental surgery the next day. I hadn't even spoken to John, yet.

I had a brief text exchange with him about my surgery, and whether or not I should still go to Phoenix that night. We agreed that I would go ahead and catch the flight; after all, I did have a huge interview lined up with an ad agency in Scottsdale, and it was an opportunity I didn't want to miss. I'd pretty much given up on my own marketing agency at this point and decided the best thing to do was join the ranks of corporate America, where at least my talents would serve a purpose.

***

My plane landed around midnight, and I took an Uber to the hotel where John was staying, right next to his company's massive complex. I grabbed the room key waiting for me at the front desk, walked up to the room; and, without even a greeting, threw my bag down and went straight to my own bed to sleep.

The next morning, I took the rental car for the day since I had an interview, and John could walk to his office from the hotel. My face was swollen, and I still had gauze rolled up inside my cheek from the surgery. I drooled my way through interviews with four different people at the agency, who all agreed (though not in these exact words) that it was pretty damn ballsy of me to go through with the meetings while looking like a baseball was protruding from my face.

John and I spent a couple days looking at places, eventually settling on a townhouse in North Phoenix. We were all set to move a couple weeks later, with Halloween just around the corner.

The Fuckery that is...

(Another) Fresh Start.

"You write your own definition of who you are. Anyone else's definition of you is merely an opinion." – Ty Paige

We drove from Dallas to Phoenix, turning the two-day journey into a mini road trip by stopping along the way at landmarks like the Prada Marfa and White Sands National Park of Dunes. I felt like we were reconnecting: actually enjoying being around each other, and (although rather boring and mundane) even having sex in the hotel!

We got all moved into our new home, which was smaller than the one we'd had in Dallas. But it seemed like we were a team again. Phoenix was beautiful, and I was loving my early morning hikes to watch the sunrise. It seemed that everyone I met, I instantly connected with. I was feeling, well, kind of *happy*.

***

I'd decided to turn down the Scottsdale position to keep growing my own agency. After all, I'd landed a big contract with a mobile company back in Dallas, which meant I got to travel there every couple of weeks. This decision would end up being a very bad one – the reason being, I ended up meeting the next guy who'd inspire several more chapters of fuckery. But all in all, things were going pretty well.

Right before Thanksgiving, I was researching vacation destinations. I'd spent all day scrolling through posts in a "Girls Love Travel" Facebook group, with Thailand and Bali solidly at the top of my list. John and I had even talked about taking a trip there together, so I was pretty optimistic.

His response when I asked him?

"No. I can't take the time off, and I already have plans for Final Four and the Vegas weekend."

You have got to be fucking kidding me. You'd rather go on a weekend bender with your guy friends, that you already do three times a year, than take a once-in-a-lifetime trip abroad with your *wife*?

Fuck you, watch this!

I found a cheap flight for the second week of December, just for me. I started planning every detail of a two-week-long trip to both Thailand and Bali: all the places I'd go, things I'd do, where I'd stay… Out of respect for our marriage, I even asked John if he had any issue with me going alone, and he didn't.

Good. I just had one more thing left to do.

I posted to my Facebook, asking friends who'd traveled there for tips and advice. For the most part, I got some great feedback; but there were, of course, some shitty, underhanded comments about traveling alone and being stupid. Even John's sister-in-law commented.

YOU. ARE. CRAZY!! This just proves it! Ha! Why in the world would you have ANY desire to travel alone? I've never understood that... Especially when you said you'd want to get there and join travel groups to meet other tourists?!?!? (crazy face emoji) That's straight up insane to me. Go with your friends! Or your husband! ☺

Oh, if only she knew. I took a deep breath before crafting my response to this bullshit.

A solo adventure is an experience I've always wanted for myself. Traveling alone forces you to get in touch with yourself, learn new things, soul search a bit and rejuvenate your purpose. Meeting travelers and tourists from all over the world is a wonderful cultural experience. I replied.

Her one-sentence reply, which felt like such a jab, was:

I don't disagree with your last statement.

I could feel her judgment as I read every word she'd not-so-eloquently typed out. This was *my* fucking life, and I was going to do what I wanted to do. Why did it matter if I wanted to go travel alone? I wasn't hurting anyone. I wasn't a housewife without a job who depended on her husband for everything, social and financial. I responded with elegance:

I've certainly met people while on vacation with friends or John before, but all American tourists in "party mode". When you're on a solo trip for the purpose of adventure, sightseeing and education, you meet different types of people with different interests. I'm very independent, yet I've never ventured out like this before. This might be exactly what I need for myself.

In retrospect, I wish I could have taken that trip when I had planned on it; but I ended up needing that time for heaps more fuckery. It would be two more years before I'd finally get to take my first big international solo trip – and get to write a book about it! Funny how things work out.

The Fuckery that is...

Thanksgiving.

"Friendship is weird. You pick a human you've met and you're like 'yep, I like this one' and you just do stuff with them." – Bill Murray

John would always win the Thanksgiving "where are we going?" battle. His family was huge, and his mom would invite everyone over for this lavish, over-the-top classic Southern meal that could feed a small country. I'd gone with him for three years now, and for some reason, this year, I didn't want to go.

I take that back – I knew *exactly* why I didn't want to go. I'd have to pay over $500 for a flight and a rental car, all to spend five days in the middle of bumfuck nowhere. I'd be bitten by ants, cook a bunch of food I didn't even like, clean up after twenty or so people, have conversations with his backstabbing family members, chase kids around who'd steal my makeup... and be ignored by my husband the entire fucking time while he played dominoes and get drunk with his brothers, cousins, and uncles.

I wanted a weekend to do whatever I wanted. I wanted to get a gas station hot dog, like I always did as a holiday tradition dating back to when I was a teenager living in my car. I wanted to watch whatever I wanted to on TV and make a couple of chunky yarn blankets for my friends as Christmas presents.

***

As luck would have it, my friend Laron, who lived in Minneapolis in Minnesota, was toying with the idea of coming to visit me for a weekend. We'd talked about it a couple times, and I thought, hey, if she wanted to visit when John wouldn't be around, why not come over for Thanksgiving! So, I fixed her a flight, and we started planning the hikes we wanted to take, some quality wine and arts-and-crafts time at my house, and, of course, good, old-fashioned hanging out.

Laron and I had met earlier that year, while I was in Austin for the South by Southwest festival (SXSW). Her sister lived there, and she'd flown down for a long weekend. We were both waiting in a *very* long line for Matthew McConaughey's SXSW talk at a two-story bar downtown – and listening to a homeless man chanting "I need milk! I need milk!" over and over and over while shaking a small box of cereal.

I finally gave in, turned to Laron and her sister, and asked them to hold my place in line.

"Sure!"

I went into the little convenience store that was no more than 50 steps from where I'd been standing in line. I bought a small carton of milk, grabbed a plastic spoon from the snack station, and handed them to the homeless man. He was so thankful – as was everyone else, I imagine, because he finally shut the fuck up about the milk.

I got back in line next to Laron, thanked her for saving my place, and she thanked me for sorting the man out. We laughed about it all as we grabbed a table at the bar for some quick lunch and a beer.

We ended up spending the entire day and night together, drinking and dancing and laughing, and even met some new friends along the way. By the end of the night, I knew I'd made a lifelong friend.

***

Laron's flight got in later on Thanksgiving Day, so I curled up on the couch with my gas station hot dog, a Reese's peanut butter Christmas tree, and watched movies. I picked her up from the airport right before sunset, and we went to the nearby Picture Rock to hike and get some photos. Back at my place, we opened a bottle of wine and started working on our blankets, chilling out and enjoying each other's company. I couldn't have asked for a better Thanksgiving.

I'd only talked to John once that day, and he told me that he and his brothers went out to the city nearby the night before. They'd gone to this little bar I'd visited with John several times in the past. It was a local hangout, so I had no doubt they'd had a good time running into old friends and catching up. He insisted that was all they did; and, since it was kind of dead, they left not long into the evening and went back to his mom's.

Laron and I spent our weekend together with plenty of trips out, including some awesome brunch and dinner dates. Her friend joined us one night, and we all went to downtown Scottsdale to check out the "midget bar" and some other fun spots. We danced our asses off while meeting folks who were visiting from all over. The weekend was perfect – just what I needed.

The Fuckery that is...

Being Disposable.

"Stop crossing oceans for people who won't jump a puddle for you." – Unknown

John was going to be home on Sunday, the same day Laron was heading back to Minneapolis. I was sad that she was leaving, but happy that I'd get to see John. I was still holding on to hope that our marriage could rekindle and survive, even though I'd spent over a year grieving what I was sure we'd lost.

I was scrolling through Facebook, waiting for John to get back, when I saw it.

Why does social media seem to always be the wrench? I'm thankful for it, though, because without it, I'd never have known just what a fucking liar my husband was.

John had been tagged in a photo that he quickly hid from his timeline, I guess as soon as his flight landed. It was a picture of him, his cousin, and a few girls at a bar, from Wednesday night. You know, the night he said he was at that one bar, and only that bar, got bored, and went home?

This picture was *not* at that bar.

Here we go *again* with the lying. I didn't fucking care if he went out, or ran into friends, past lovers, past fuckbuddies, female friends, whoever! I did *not* fucking care – I just wanted him to stop. Fucking. Lying about it! Was that so much to ask? When he'd lie about it, of *course* I'd suspect he'd done something he shouldn't.

If you don't have anything to hide, you don't hide anything. Simple.

I felt myself, at long last, totally check out from this crapfest of a marriage. But first, I had to confront him. We got into an argument, *again*, because he couldn't just admit the lie and say he was sorry.

What happened the next day officially stamped my freedom passport.

***

Curiosity got the best of me. I logged into our cell service account to see who John had been texting that night. Within minutes, I got a text from him.

Why did you log into our account?

Huh? How did he know? Well, apparently, when you constantly fuck up and are paranoid about getting caught, you can take advantage of a feature that alerts you any time someone accesses your call log. This is something I'd never have thought to do, I guess because I didn't have anything to hide. Even when I was back in Detroit, visiting friends and family without him, and I spent the night at one of my guy friend's apartments, I called John to tell him I was there. That's the kind of transparency I wanted because it created trust.

After a couple messages back and forth, I told him I was checking to see who he had been texting. He shot back a few angry, mean jabs at me. I wasn't even hurt any more, I was just waiting for the shoe to drop. And boy, did it.

Why are you treating me like I'm disposable? I asked. I'm your wife.

I saw the three dots in the little bubble, as John typed the final line that would end it all.

You've earned the title of disposable.

I was enraged at the audacity of this man. To tell me this most horrific fucking thing you could ever say to a human being – even more so, your significant other. I packed my suitcase and booked a flight to Dallas for that night, then got the fuck out of there. Finally, *for good.*

***

The next morning, I woke up at Shelly's place, got on my computer, and filed for divorce. Thankfully, I hadn't yet changed my place of residency to Arizona and was able to get a 60-day divorce since I was still a Texas resident.

Every single BAC moment I'd experienced throughout my marriage got thrown into my snow globe – I didn't have the energy to waste on any of those beliefs or thoughts.

I smashed that shit-snow with all my strength against the tree, then had the best week I possibly could with my supportive friends in Dallas.

The Fuckery that is...

Butterflies.

"It's fuck-this-shit o'clock!" – Unknown

I was free. Free to do whatever I wanted. I had decisions to make, and I loved feeling in control of my future again. Did I want to stay in Phoenix, or move back to Dallas, or maybe even go to Chicago? Or would it be best to just head home to Detroit, where I could be supported by close friends and family if I needed it? I spent the next week and a half weighing all the options while traveling to see friends. Everyone said I was glowing, and how happy I looked to be free of him.

Taking the first steps, I went ahead and looked at a couple of places to rent in Detroit. If I did decide to settle down there, I wanted to be in the city proper. The downtown district had changed so much over the last ten years: it was bustling with shops, art, museums, parks, bars, and restaurants, with sports and other local events happening every weekend. My realtor showed me a townhouse first, but it was so small, I had to tell her it wasn't right for me.

"Well, I do have a studio that just listed," she said. "It's a little more than what you said you want to spend, though."

I'd always wanted to live in one of those big, open, artist's-loft-style studios smack dab in the center of Manhattan. But New York was, sadly, not an option for me, though; so, I thought, *What the hell, let's take a look at it!*

We pulled up to the building, situated in the midtown area, and took the elevator to the second floor. We turned the corner in the hallway, and she opened the door to apartment 201. I don't even think I made it further than about ten steps in before I exclaimed: "It's perfect. I'll take it!"

My new home was 900 square feet, open from end to end with space all the way to the ceiling. A large bathroom was tucked away to the right as soon as you entered, and a walk-in closet sat to the left. The kitchen and sleeping area were directly across from each other; a huge, cement martini pillar separated the spaces between the three areas; and the main living area was *huge*. It had exposed ducts, a crooked red and brown brick wall on one side, and a cement floor that had been painted in such a way to almost say "I don't give a fuck".

Interestingly enough, that was going to be my attitude for the next year.

My imagination ran wild as I mentally decorated the apartment. This bad ass fucking studio was going to be mine – *mine!* – to do pretty much whatever I wanted with. There was even a small balcony, suspended just outside the floor-to-ceiling windows, which would become my favorite spot to watch the snow fall on winter days.

I signed the lease, paid the deposit, and started planning my move.

***

A week later, I was back in Phoenix. I only had two days to separate all my belongings from John's, pack, and get the truck loaded. I'd had the mobile company I was working with help get everything set up, so my pod would end up on a trailer that was already heading to Detroit. I threw away so much stuff I had in storage bins in the garage. It was super-therapeutic to purge all the shit I just didn't need.

During the countless hours I spent in the garage, I came across my childhood bible. Tucked away inside it, I found that shitty little bookmark I mentioned earlier – the one with my biological father's eulogy on it – and that piss-sad letter from his wife (my stepmom, I guess, what the fuck). I took a few minutes to reflect on them, and what I was currently going through. It seemed to line up to one conclusion. Let's go BAC!

Belief: The men in your life have always disregarded you.

Action: This is what you are comfortable with, and why you attract men who cannot be there for you, emotionally or physically.

Challenge: Focus on yourself and have regard for your own life, fuck any commitment from men for a while. It's too heavy for you to carry as you step into a new chapter of life.

I stopped packing for a moment to look at a list I'd always kept on my phone called "Good Things". In it, I noted all the good things I did, and had done, for others, and used it as a reminder that I was needed and appreciated.

The fact was, being married to this man drained me of my happiness so much that re-reading little notes of encouragement and quotes was often one of the only ways I could get through the day. I wasn't perfect – God knows I fucked up all the time, and still sometimes do – but this little list always let me know that, even with my imperfections, I was a damn good person.

***

It was Wednesday, and, when I finally emerged from the garage, John asked me if I wanted to go to dinner. *Fuck yes!* I mean, why not get one last meal out of the asshole?

We jumped into his Jeep, the same Jeep we'd once spent time cruising around in with Bula in the back seat and venturing out to volleyball games. Then we drove the mile or so to a little restaurant-and-bar we'd visited a handful of times during the last month. To my surprise, we didn't argue, or even discuss the divorce at all. I'm not sure how we both managed to keep it so casual and fun, but we did.

The next day, I was at the cell phone store to get my service moved to my own account. While I was there, a text from John popped up.

I had a great time with you last night. Hope we can continue to keep things cordial.

For one, single split second, I felt butterflies in my stomach all over again, just like I did at the very beginning. I started to cry, right there in the middle of the store. I felt crazy for having any feelings after everything this douche had put me through.

I called Shelly as soon as I left. She reassured me that I was doing the right thing, and even said to me: "Remember, Ty. Fingers and toes."

She was right. I needed to stay true to being completely checked out of this marriage. Whatever sociopathic move he was trying to make could no longer affect me. I was done with him, with the way he had treated me, and with everything he pretended to be.

He was nothing more than a John Doe. He wasn't real – hence, his pseudonym in this book.

The Fuckery that is...

A Bachelor Party.

"There is a voice that doesn't use words. Listen." - RUMI

Friday rolled around, with the movers set to arrive at 9:00 AM. John was preparing to leave for Vegas for the weekend, and I'd also woken up early to get ready for what was to be an emotionally draining day. Not because this'd be the last time I'd see John, but because about an hour after he took off, I got a phone call that confirmed every single fucking gut feeling I'd ever had about his lies and unfaithfulness.

John gave me a pitiful goodbye hug by the first-floor door next to the garage. As he walked away across the parking lot, out of my life forever, I couldn't help but feel a touch of sadness. This was it. The marriage I'd fought so fucking hard to save was officially over, and there was no turning back.

I was standing in the mostly empty living room. The couch – a gorgeous, custom-made piece I'd ordered just a few weeks prior – was already loaded up. I couldn't wait to get that oversized embodiment of comfort into my new place and chill out on the huge chaise!

If you're wondering why I didn't snag any of John's furniture, I'd already sold the raggedy-ass couch and loveseat through Facebook Marketplace. Of course, he didn't offer to help at all, or really seem to give a shit. He just took the $300 cash, didn't even think to throw it toward the cost of the replacement. Maybe, deep down, I knew that new couch was meant to be all mine.

My phone rang, and I picked up to find one of John's friends calling me.

"Hey, you doing okay?" they asked. "Not sure if today's the day you're officially moving."

"Yeah, the movers are here now. I'm actually doing pretty good. John just left for Vegas. Feeling optimistic. How are you guys?"

"Glad to hear it. You're doing the right thing." A pause. "You have no idea – the things I know he did behind your back."

"Oh, really?" I was pissed John's buddy hadn't warned me about all this shit earlier; but I had to admit I was curious, too. "Now's a good time to tell me. He's gone, and I'm moving on."

"Okay... Well, this past summer. We were out having drinks with Will one night, and it came up that he'd had those girls over. Will was like, 'Oh my God, seriously? He's doing it again?'. We asked him what he meant, and he told us everything about the bachelor party. He said that John had a threesome with a couple of, uh, larger girls they'd brought back to the house in Scottsdale."

"Wow. I fucking knew it."

My heart dropped further and further as John's friend revealed everything they'd heard that went down at the bachelor party (which, weirdly enough, had taken place just a few miles from where I was standing). When we hung up, I decided to call Will and ask straight up what happened. After all, Will was actually there at the bachelor party, so I was pretty confident I could trust what he said.

"Hello?" he answered.

"Hey, Will. I have a question for you. This isn't going to be a fun conversation, but it's going to be real. I need to know."

"Okay, shoot."

"Did John really have a threesome with two girls at his bachelor party?"

I heard a sigh on the other end of the phone. He really didn't need to say any more – but he did, telling me about one of the other guys who'd been involved in the orgy as well. That was fucked up because the guy in question was *married to my friend.* They'd even asked Will if he wanted to join, as they went into the room near his to engage in a little pre-marital/marital foursome, but he'd declined. And to think John came home the next day and kissed me! *Gross.*

Usually, I was able to keep my anger in check, calm down enough to stay rational. But not now. Not with this information. *Why the fuck did he marry me if he wanted to be single?* I thought.

I texted John.

Why did you even marry me after fucking those girls at your bachelor party?

John texted back immediately.

What? What are you talking about?

You can't hide the truth anymore. I know what you did. I can't believe you married me after doing that.

His gaslighting-as-all-fuck reply?

This is exactly why I want a divorce.

All I could do was roll my eyes and force myself not to take the baseball bat beside me to his prized possession, a 70" 3D HDTV. Instead, I grabbed the wooden box that contained all of the little things we'd collected as "love memories" and dumped them out all over the floor.

The poor guys that were working so hard to move my stuff down two flights of stairs had to witness my sheer anger, and they even commented that, in their opinion, I was holding myself together way better than most would. Good thing that these three strapping young men were so unbelievably nice, because they'd end up being my emotional crutch for the next hour or so.

I watched as they wrapped up and loaded my easel, the final thing destined for the removal truck. Then I loaded up my car with my suitcase, air mattress, blankets, pillows, and my most precious possession, Bula girl, and got the fuck out of there.

The Fuckery that is...

The Grand Canyon.

"There's a time and place for everything. But, as I get older, I like finding those human moments and really connecting." – Paul Walker

I'd booked a hotel in Phoenix for that night because I wasn't sure if I'd be ready to hit the road just yet. After getting an oil change and some thorough maintenance on my Lexus SUV – like fuck was I going to break down during the over-2,000-mile drive to Detroit! – I checked into the room and watched some TV, trying to relax and get my mind off everything. I'd ordered in some food, too, which was fucking pointless because I had no appetite. In the end, decided I'd take myself out for some drinks.

Fuck it, you deserve it!

My first stop, after leaving Phoenix, was the Grand Canyon. I'd never been there before, and, since it wasn't too far off my route to Detroit, of course I couldn't miss the chance! Driving around the canyon itself was a bit of a slog, but it was all worth it once I reached the South Rim.

As Bula and I stood there, I realized that this natural formation, with its millions of years of history, had given me some serious clarity. With miles upon miles of carved, perfectly uneven beauty, it didn't even seem real. It felt as if I could just reach my hand out over it to touch it, like a painting.

I had an epiphany – not a BAC, but an actual epiphany. What I was staring at was so much like my marriage. It was picture-perfect on the surface, but if you dove deep, it was nothing but layers of imperfections: dingy dirt, red mud that will stain you, sharp rocks, and danger. If you weren't careful, you could be seriously hurt.

***

My next few days of driving across the country were filled with unexpected adventures. Among many, many other places, I stopped at the Four Corners of America monument, where Arizona, Colorado, New Mexico, and Utah meet; an antique shop with a huge rooster statue out front (I just had to get a picture with the massive cock); and a small town in La Platte, Nebraska, where I met some locals at a little dive bar. I made sure to hit any little touristy spot along the way, too. By Monday, I was ready to be home, so I pushed through the remaining fifteen or so hours until I arrived in Detroit. It was Christmas Eve.

I spent the next few days with family and friends, bombarded by questions from all sides about what had gone wrong in my marriage. I tried to stay positive and focused on my future, but it was tough when I was still getting messages and calls from people who knew John – and about his indiscretions.

His ex-girlfriend even reached out, telling me about that weekend he had gone back to his hometown without me (you know, when he left me crying in the bathroom, then called me at 3:00 AM). She'd seen him making out with a girl they both knew at the bar, then leaving with her.

I'd also learned about a coworker of his in Detroit, and how everyone at the office had suspected something was going on between them. The girl involved had quite a reputation: as the wife of one of John's colleagues explained, she'd caught her having an affair with her husband. Amanda, the first girl I'd mentioned on the fingers and toes count, messaged me as well, admitting that she and John had been having sex when he and I had first started dating.

Another couple we'd befriended in Dallas texted me about seeing John in their neighborhood a few times. Apparently, they knew he'd done cocaine the few times we'd all hung out at the neighbor's parties. They also knew I was against it and didn't want to ruffle feathers. But now that I had left him, they came clean. The truth was, the couple that would host these crazy pool parties were huge cokeheads; and another neighbor, Erika, was the supplier. She had a slutty vibe about her, so it's likely she and John were snorting coke and banging. I'll never know for sure, but my gut feeling was probably right.

***

Will called me a few days after he'd confirmed the bachelor party fuck-fest with a complaint of his own.

"Hey Will, what's up?" I said.

"I'm just… *so* fucking annoyed with John."

"Why, what happened?"

"He's calling me, and everyone else who was on the bachelor party trip, asking who ratted him out and if we're all 'still cool' with him," Will seethed. "I'm thinking, dude, you don't even give a shit about the fact you cheated and lied! You haven't called me to ask how I'm doing, or how my family's doing, in over a year, but you get busted and now you want to make sure we're chill? I'm just… over it."

"Oh my gosh. I'm so sorry."

"Seriously, Ty. You've called and texted me way more than he has since we've known each other."

"I swear, I haven't told one single person who it was who let me know about the party," I insisted. "It wasn't even you. But I promised them that I'd never tell. It doesn't even matter anymore. It's over."

"You're too good for that. You're so much better off without him. John will always be a *friend* of mine because we have so much history, but it'll never be the same. I've lost all respect for him."

***

I bet you're also wondering what the fuck was up with that totally-not-coke he'd totally not asked for in Mexico. It's probably obvious by now, but he'd been scoring for the entire trip, so the poor guy who I scolded for trying to hand off the little baggy to me was probably very confused.

And, in the coming months of traveling back and forth to Dallas for work, Hattie herself would reveal that she and John were doing coke every time they hung out. I guess that's why it was so easy for them to party until 10 AM – and yet another reason why he'd spend so long in the fucking bathroom!

The secrets didn't stop there. Turned out they'd partied at my house while I was in Saint Maarten, and John boasted to Hattie that he'd slept with *over 300 women*.

Who was this complete other person that I'd married? I swear to God, I just wanted to scream.

The divorce would be final on February 20th, and it couldn't come soon enough. I'd gone to the doctor to get tested for STDs, and learned he'd removed me from our health insurance, which is straight-up illegal. I sent him a strongly worded email with the facts, as well as mentioning that I knew about the rampant cheating.

You can pay your own bills through the divorce.

That – was all he wrote back.

Well, shit. The separation orders said not to make any changes to existing, shared accounts at all. I couldn't even get my name taken off the lease in Phoenix until we'd officially divorced!

The Fuckery that is...

Back to the Future.

"If you want the rainbow, you gotta put up with the rain." –
Dolly Parton

The trailer with all of my belongings rocked up on a Saturday, so
I hightailed it to my new studio with my friend Josh in tow. Once
everything was tossed carelessly inside, there were at least thirty
boxes stacked from floor to ceiling in the middle of the open space,
like some sort of cardboard Everest. No fucking way was I
tackling that climb now – I was too exhausted and overwhelmed
by the prospect. Instead, we decided to go next door to the trendy
Hopcat bar for a couple cold beers and some burgers.

***

Remember Josh? He and I had been friends for about nine years
at this point. We first met in the fall of 2011, when I was dating a
guy named Mack, and before I'd even glimpsed the douchebag
who would later become my husband. Although Josh and I had an
instant connection over music, specifically Johnny Cash's "Hurt",
we kept a degree of distance in our friendship until I became single
the following year.

In a twist I'm sure will shock none of you, I'd caught Mack cheating on me with one of his customers the week of my birthday. And so, after nearly three years together, I packed and moved into my own apartment with the ultimate quickness.

Mack was an odd one. He'd pay $30 a month for anal fisting porn; He was obsessed with anal sex. I wasn't interested myself, but man, would he try and convince me! He even bought me butt toys for Christmas one year – which I ended up having a blast with once I found out he was cheating. The woman he'd gone off with knew he had a girlfriend, and, of course, decided to go ahead and fuck him anyway. She was having an open house that weekend, so I took my private investigator skills to the next level, finding out where she lived. I scattered those toys all over her lawn just as the viewing was about to begin. Hey, she'd *ass*-ked for it!

Anyway, back to Josh. He and I shared a birthday, so after I got settled into my new apartment, I'd invited him to go out and party with our thirty or so mutual friends. After a few hours of drinking and dancing, we took a taxi back to my place, just us two – and, somewhere en route, without even a word, we looked at each other and started making out. We ended up having amazing sex all night (seriously, I had bruises!). It was passionate, and *oh so good*.

We hooked up a few more times over the next month. Our friends-with-benefits arrangement was ideal for me, because we knew we weren't interested in anything more from each other. The sex was always mind-blowing, and I enjoyed the time we spent together outside the bedroom, too. I even met Josh's family, who instantly made me feel like one of their own.

By the end of April, with the sparks dissolved, we were back to being strictly friends. In a super weird way that, really, makes no sense at all, Josh became more like a brother to me than a past lover. I was thankful we were able to go back to that dynamic, because both he and his family are incredibly dear to me.

***

With the last bites of our food eaten and our beers downed, I was more than ready to spend my first night – alone! – in my new studio. I flopped down on the couch with my cozy, chunky yarn blanket I had made over Thanksgiving wrapped around me and fell fast asleep.

I was back in Detroit, and everything felt perfect.

The Fuckery that is...

New Year's.

"Laughter is the sound of your heart smiling." – Ty Paige

I'd asked my good friend Jess – a die-hard Green Bay Packers fan – to go with me to their upcoming game versus the Detroit Lions. Of course, she was thrilled; and the break from taking care of her two-year-old little boy would be an added bonus!

Since it was frigid cold outside, and that mile long walk would have left us unable to feel our toes, we took an Uber together to the stadium, where we met up with some other friends who were hosting mini tailgate parties and barhopping. We also ran into a guy we'd played football with back in school, with whom we were still good buddies.

The three of us ended up hanging out the rest of the day, even going over to the Elwood Bar after the game for a few drinks. Little surprise that we found Terry Foster there – my former CBS Radio coworker (and long-time buddy) – who had become quite a local celebrity through hosting his sports radio talk show. He'd never turn down an invite to have a beer and watch a game with me, always saying, "Ty, you know more about football than most guys!" As usual – and, as often happened when just Terry and I met up – people kept approaching him, not wanting to miss the photo opportunity!

***

Evening came, and we went our separate ways. Well, Jess did – I headed back to my place with our old football friend.

The new bed I'd ordered had been delivered to the lobby of my building. And so together, we carried it into my still-cluttered studio, all buzzed up from day drinking, laughing hysterically about how clumsy this attempt to construct it was going to be. We soon said a mutual "fuck that" to the idea, instead only taking out the bed-in-a-box mattress.

We sliced open the clear plastic bag, watched it take shape – and fell on top of it, arms around each other, for some good, old-fashioned fooling around. Holy fuck, I'd forgotten how much fun it was to just *make out.* I'd been deprived of any real intimacy in my marriage, and anything remotely resembling it was *way* overdue.

Then again, I guess that was a lot to ask of a guy who was too busy lying and sticking his dick in other girls. Asshole.

***

It took two full days to completely unpack and get everything in place in my new apartment. I wasn't entirely sure why I'd kept my wedding dress. But, as I hung it up on the closet door, I couldn't help thinking how gorgeous it was, with all that intricate beading and lace and layers of grungy netting at the bottom. It was the perfect combination of the more traditional outfit John had wanted to see, and what I wanted to feel – unique and a bit off-trend. Shit, if it had been totally up to me, my dress would have been off-white with pink and green embroidered flowers, like I'd seen on a 2008 episode of *Say Yes to the Dress*!

I stood there for a good long while, wondering what to do with the thing now that it stood for absolutely nothing.

***

8:00 PM, New Year's Eve. I looked around at my new place, with everything perfectly situated, exactly as I'd imagined when I'd first stepped into the empty space, and let out a sigh. After all the bullshit I'd had to deal with, I was *beyond* ready for a new year.

I didn't have any plans to go out that night, so I cracked open a cold beer and drank it while I cooked a tasty (and deliciously cheap) frozen pizza. I settled in on the couch and finished the whole thing while taking full advantage of Netflix's final night to stream *Friends*.

Was it just a coincidence, or some cosmic fuckery that woke me right after midnight? I have no clue, but I do know I was awake just long enough to tell myself:

"Happy New Year, Ty."

The Fuckery that is...

23 & Me.

"Imperfection is beauty, madness is genius, and it's better to be absolutely ridiculous than absolutely boring." – Marilyn Monroe

It didn't take long for everyone I knew in Detroit to catch wind of my new single status. Not that I'd made any secret of it, but it was pretty obvious they'd figured it out when guys I'd made friends with through various sports started hitting me up! Football jocks, kickball boys, volleyball dudes – you name it, they were sliding into my DMs. I wasn't ready to date at all, but I was debating the idea of getting some action here and there. Fuck it, why not?

One of the messages was from this guy, Darren, a tall-dark-and-handsome athletic type who played football with John. He was very obviously flirting with me, straight-up asking if he could come and see me soon. I looked at the picture of his tousled hair, his perfect features and sculpted figure (kinda like the surfer guy in the café story). I smiled to myself.

Sure! Come on down any time! I replied.

***

Indeed, he did, showing up a couple days later on a Friday. We chilled in my living room, had a beer, and chatted about everything that had gone wrong in my marriage. Darren was super-compassionate, sharing my confusion over John's behavior – after all, from the sidelines, we'd seemed like a fairytale couple.

Darren hadn't known I was with John when he first saw me, and he admitted he'd asked his friend "Who is *that?*", in a "holy shit, she's hot!" kind of way. He even recalled exactly what I was wearing – pink shorts and a white tank top – which I found really endearing. Now, though, single Ty was sitting in front of him, and he wanted to make his move.

"Wait a second," I said, as he leaned in towards me. "How old are you?"

Darren was one of those guys whose age you just couldn't tell. Twenty-five? Thirty-five? Both would be excellent guesses.

"Twenty-three," he answered.

Oh, dear God. I asked him how old his parents were, found out his mother was six months younger than me! What the fuck, Ty? Are you really about to go *there?*

Yep, I sure did! Why not? This was my time to have some non-committal fun. Yeah, he might have only been 23, but he was mature and showed a lot of empathy. We hooked up pretty frequently for about 3 weeks, and it was awesome every. Single. Fucking. Time.

Darren would even call me while I was traveling for work, and whenever I went to see friends or colleagues, he'd ask me to tell them "hello" from him. I really liked how he was always so polite and kind. Obviously, this wasn't going to turn into anything of romantic substance, though he *did* try to tell me, once, that he was falling for me. Uh, no, dude, you're not! I'm not going there, and neither are you. This was just for fun. Thanks for the sex, thanks for the attention and the ego boost and being so understanding about my fucked-up ex, but, just, *nope*. I'm out!

The Fuckery that is...

Destroying the Dress.

"Life is, oddly, fucking beautiful." – Ty Paige

Since Thailand and Bali never got to happen, I was determined to take a solo trip to Cancun for a few days to escape the winter and reset my mind. When Josh found out, though, he said I was absolutely not going alone, and asked if he could join me. Eh, why not? We always had fun together.

There was only one more thing left to do (aside from the divorce, of course) to free myself of John's bullshit forever. My stupid wedding dress was still hanging there, staring me down, shooting little eye-daggers of disappointment at me every time I walked past it. I'd finally decided what I wanted to do with it. In true artist fashion, I was going to utterly destroy it and have my friend Colin do a photoshoot.

I laid out an old sheet to protect the colorful, pixel-pattern rug from the approaching onslaught. I threw the damn dress on top of it and snatched up several bottles of paint from behind my easel. I tore the caps off the colors, one by one.

I took aim, gripping a bottle in each hand, and prepared to fuck shit up.

"Liar! Cheater! Cokehead, narcissist, traitor…!" I screamed all the derogatory names I could find for John as they came to mind, whipping my arms wildly, watching slashes of paint fly through the air and land on the dress. Each new mark on the fabric was like a colorful scar, a way John had hurt me that I was leaving behind.

About three minutes later, I was done. I took a step back, panting, to gaze upon my masterpiece. It was, oddly, fucking beautiful; more *me* than the original dress had ever been.

John had spent two years destroying our marriage; and, in no time at all, almost two years to the exact date of our wedding, I'd destroyed the memory of the day I now called the "Mexican mistake".

***

Colin, who was a highly talented and well-known Detroit photographer, arrived at my studio an hour later. For the first set of photos, I lay on the floor, using my pixel rug as a backdrop. Then, I donned my new dress, grabbed a beer from the refrigerator, and posed with it on my beloved oversized couch for a couple shots of me in my own, happy-as-fuck element.

After some more inside shots, we went out to the street. Colin snapped away as I walked past a brick building with huge, loudly painted murals, down the alley behind my apartment block, and into the busy streets of downtown Detroit.

I quickly changed into a black dress, black heels and dark

sunglasses, appropriate for the death of this fucking marriage. Time for the grand finale. With sunglasses and a drink in hand, and my destroyed dress slung over my arm, we made our way down to a viaduct whose graffitied wall, rather fittingly, declared *Danger, Reality Ahead.* We staged a few pictures there, then walked over to a nearby abandoned building. Just outside sat a huge stone fire pit, where the local homeless folks often gathered to get some warmth.

Colin and I got our own fire going. I took a sip of my 40 oz. Miller High Life – what better drink to take back my own life with? – then tossed the dress into the flames without a care in the world.

We stood there, watching as my $7,000 Kleinfeld wedding dress* burned to ashes.

*I made a monetary donation to the Little Angel Gowns foundation in honor of my dress since they weren't in immediate need of physical products. Little Angel Gowns is a non-profit organization that uses donated wedding dresses to make outfits for babies and toddlers who have, tragically, passed away.

The Fuckery that is...

COVID.

"What a year this week has been." – Unknown

After Josh and I returned from our all-inclusive Cancun vacation, I took my final trip to Dallas for work – and to appear before a judge to finalize the divorce. I literally danced my ass out of the courtroom when the hearing was over!

It was February 18th, 2020, two days earlier than I'd expected.

I'd told everyone at the office, as well as all my Dallas friends (which included some of John's buddies) that we'd be celebrating my divorce that night. About twenty people showed up, and I even did a shot of tequila, something I'd always reserved for roughly three special occasions a year, including my birthday. I mean, my custom-made shirt *did* direct me to *Take a shot, I untied the knot!*

***

Two days later, I was walking past the conference room at the mobile company's office when I had another movie-worthy guy moment. The man sitting behind the glass, looking right at me, was strikingly handsome, although his facial features were larger than what society would accept on someone traditionally "hot". His smile was warm, inviting, lighting up his oddly perfect face; he had an air of almost unbearable cuteness.

We exchanged dreamy-eyed glances. Time seemed to slow down – so much that I came to a stop in the corridor.

Now, I'd seen this guy pop up in that "people you may know" section of Facebook. I vividly remembered that when I saw his face, mostly because I'd thought, *Shit, I wish I knew him,* when I'd first seen his profile pic. He'd definitely selected the best photo of himself, and it was an accurate depiction of his IRL appearance.

I entered the conference room, which was filled with about ten guys all in training to be estimators. Blake (as I will call him, for reasons you'll see later) and I exchanged a few sentences; and instantly, I felt he was my type of guy.

We became friends on Facebook, staying in touch for a few months. He lived in a big city down south, and I lived in Detroit, so visiting each other in person was pretty much out of the question thanks to the impending COVID-19 pandemic. We didn't communicate much, anyway – just some flirty comments on each other's posts and an occasional FaceTime drink together, and of course those first memorable few minutes of flirty office conversation.

Amidst the quarantines and travel restrictions that would soon sweep the world, it was no big deal that's all we could do. It's not like we had anything serious… yet.

Fair warning: little did I know that Blake would turn out to be a monster. It's funny how quickly someone can diminish from being the most gorgeous person you've ever laid eyes on to nothing more than a disgusting shell, a truly sad excuse for a human. When you finally meet the person they really are on the inside, it becomes all you can see on the outside. And after what Blake would end up doing to me – and what I'd learn he'd done to other women – he's now nothing more than a pile of white trash to me.

***

Anyway… My divorce having been finalized two days prior; I was stoked as hell to be legally free from the man I thought was one of the *worst* human beings in the world. I was happy to be free from the past, ecstatic to be getting my life back on track and spending some time doing whatever *I* wanted. No man to worry about, no constant fights over his cheating, lying, gaslighting, and manipulating. I was just… happy.

That was until the world started going to shit. Luckily, I'd made it back to Detroit before the lockdowns started in earnest. I, like many others, watched helplessly as events were cancelled, restaurants were closed, and people got sick from one side of the planet all the way to the other.

At first, I felt nervous about the pandemic. I wouldn't leave my studio much at all, and every time I'd order groceries or food, the drivers would leave everything outside my door, using a new method called "contactless delivery". Careful as I was, it didn't stop me from catching COVID in early March.

The symptoms only lasted a couple of days, but I couldn't taste shit, and I suffered with splitting headaches, a low grade-fever, and body aches that were so severe my limbs would jolt uncontrollably. I'd already been quarantining alone, bored out of my fucking mind, and now I was going to have to spend *another* two weeks couped up in my one room studio.

What the fuck?

I wanted to lock myself inside my walk-in closet and scream as loud as I could. But I decided to take the more constructive route, heading up to the rooftop of my building at least once a day to take in the open air and views of the city. I'd even (illegally) climb the huge, rusted water tower up there, just to feel alive. From the top, you could see clear to Windsor, Ontario in neighboring Canada.

St. Patrick's Day in downtown Detroit was, traditionally, a massive celebration, when head-to-toe-green-dressed people from all over the suburbs would gather in the streets, downing green beer, dipping in and out of bars and restaurants, accompanied by upbeat tunes courtesy of local musicians. It was the last big downtown bash before the Detroit Tigers' opening day – and damn, Detroit knew how to fucking party on the first day of baseball season, possibly even putting Boston to shame.

That year, though? I only saw about ten people, and maybe twenty other vehicles, on the 15-minute drive I took to escape my apartment for a little while. File that under "one of the most depressing experiences of my life".

***

Unfortunately, my birthday was just a couple weeks away, falling smack-dab in the middle of this quarantine fuckery. We'd all been ordered to stay home, so I hadn't planned anything at all, which sucked monumentally since I'd always made a big deal about what was, essentially, my own personal holiday. My biological family had never done much for traditional celebrations like Christmas or Easter, and party-focused holidays – any excuse to let loose! – had quickly become my favorites.

Feeling much better, and having spent barely any time outside my studio, I figured it was safe to invite a friend over for my birthday.

Colin rode his bike over from his home downtown and spent at least an hour setting up my surprise party. He asked me to dress up, just as if we were going out somewhere, and I had the bright idea to get dolled up in an 80's throwback style (think Kelly Kapowski in *Saved by the Bell*!). I dug deep into my closet, grabbing a skintight mini floral dress, jean jacket, and some hot pink flats, completing the look with bright blue eyeshadow and hot pink lipstick – and, of course, a rhinestone tiara. Colin walked me up to the rooftop with a Bluetooth speaker in hand, where we proceeded to have a truly epic rooftop club party in the freezing-cold air.

It was the best birthday I could have imagined, given the state of everything.

***

April, for the most part, kind of breezed by me. I joined TikTok, making the first of those hilarious, short-form videos exposing John's lies, and followed several dance trends in an effort to keep busy and get some much-needed exercise. I'd also get together with my "pseudo" family once a week for dinner and drinks at my "sister" Kelly's place, taking advantage of the chance to surround myself with familiar faces, laughs, and all-round good company.

These folks had quickly become my real family, after I first met them back in 2007. Liz (mom) worked at a marketing agency I used to freelance for. She was a tall, 50-something, stunningly gorgeous blonde with a perfect tan, and a ripe personality that made everyone love her instantly.

While working a Thanksgiving charity event, she'd introduced me to her husband, Sam; and, seeing that I had no people of my own to celebrate with, they'd invited me to join them for dinner. I initially declined, but after a couple more invitations to various holiday parties, I said, "fuck it" and decided to go to the next one.

I met their children, Kelly and Nick, who were both close to me in age, and all of their amazing friends and family – uncles, aunts, cousins. Sam and Liz referred to me as their "third kid" by the end of the night, after rounds of drinking games, storytelling, and cracking up at Sam's dad jokes.

It was the best invite I ever RSVP'd "yes" to.

The Fuckery that is...

No Work.

*"Sometimes it's **not** about the journey, but yet it **is** about the destination." – Ty Paige*

May came, and I was *so* over this COVID bullshit. Airlines had finally started opening up their normal travel routes; so, I decided to fly down to Dallas to surprise Shelly with a weekend visit. I enlisted the help of our mutual friend, Christy, who offered to pick me up when I landed.

Keeping this all under wraps was going to be a little tricky, because Shelly and I talked on the phone every single day, sometimes for hours. I'd have to find a damn good excuse to miss our usual morning call, what with my flight leaving early – but I had a couple ideas.

***

I dialed Shelly's number as soon as I got to Christy's, telling her I'd had a busy morning and didn't realize my phone was off, even going so far as to exclaim how cold it was out on my balcony in Detroit. Shelly didn't question it, and I thought I was in the clear

– until a huge fucking plane flew over, engines roaring as it took off from the nearby airport. Oh, shit! I hit the mute button as fast as I could. Everyone was supposed to be working from home unless they were in healthcare or travel.

I waited, praying that I wasn't busted. Shelly continued talking about her workday; and, when the danger had passed and I swung back into the conversation, it was like nothing out of the ordinary had happened. Thank God, she was still blissfully unaware.

An hour or so later, Christy texted Shelly, saying she had something to drop off at her place. We hopped in her car right after, driving over to Shelly's building and heading up to her second-floor apartment.

I handed my phone to Christy to video Shelly's reaction and knocked.

A few seconds passed. There were footsteps inside the apartment, the click of the lock. The door swung open, revealing Shelly, who took one look at me and said:

"No. Fucking. Way!"

We hugged and hugged as tears filled our eyes. This was the longest we'd gone without seeing each other since we'd met back in 2018, and we never wanted to be separated like that again.

***

For two days straight, we just hung out: eating, drinking, playing games. We sat with Christy by her pool, laughing at the memories we'd made together on our vacation in Saint Maarten. Christy's boyfriend did a decent job of letting us have our girl time, but we didn't mind when he joined in now and then.

On Saturday night, we'd all gathered around their huge dining room table, which was perfect for entertaining, and got a few card and party games going. I'd invited Alex, a guy friend I played volleyball the previous summer, to come over. Alex was a younger guy, about thirty-three, with dark hair, dark eyes, and sun-kissed Mexican skin. He drove a stick-shift Mustang, which was such a damn turn-on. I don't know about you, but I think a man who can drive a manual is just so fucking hot! He even let me take it for a spin around the neighborhood when he first got to Christy's.

A couple of our other girlfriends had invited their significant others to join in on the evening fun, so there were about ten of us, all in all. We laughed our way through round after round of charades, Cards Against Humanity – both recipes for a fantastic night – and a game where you had to guess how someone would react to a situation posed on the card they were dealt. My stomach hurt so fucking bad, I was practically splitting my sides over some of the insane responses!

Alex was getting ready to leave, and, with a set of balls on him like no other, asked me to go home with him. Conflicted, I pulled Shelly into a corner, saying, "Oh God, this is a bad idea." I knew if I said yes, it was going to be an all-night fiasco of drunken, sloppy sex.

And it sure was.

***

When I woke up the next morning, I looked over at Alex and

shook my head. Oh, Lord. Had I really gone home with my friend and fucked him? I glanced over at his dresser. My clothes were sitting on top, unfolded, like they'd been carelessly thrown up there. I tried not to let my OCD force me to get up and fold them properly, or, shit, put them back on.

Alex opened his big, beautiful brown eyes.

"Good morning, beautiful," he said, wrapping his arm around me.

"Good morning."

"Last night was fun!"

"Yeah, it was…!"

Ding, ding, ding! Get ready for round two!

An hour and two more sex sessions later, we got dressed and he took me back to Shelly's. He gave me a huge, unexpected hug before he left. It lasted about thirty seconds, and I couldn't help thinking how different it felt to John's last, pathetic attempt at an embrace. Here was this guy, eight or so years my junior, treating me the way a genuine, kind man should treat a woman.

We said goodbye, agreeing to stay in touch.

"Don't judge me!" I laughed as I walked in the door.

"No worse than 23 & Me!" Shelly shot back.

We giggled like teenagers, like we always did when our private nickname for Darren got brought up. It'd come from me sending

Shelly the logo for that 23andMe DNA testing company any time she'd called, and I was, ahem, busy with Darren.

Who the fuck did I think I was, at forty-one years old, having sex with these young guys? I guess since I still looked pretty good for my age, I decided I didn't really give a shit. I was living my best single life!

Over the next month, Alex and I talked regularly, and he'd planned to come visit me in Detroit in June. I'd planned all kinds of fun things for us to do, which, naturally, included much more hot sex. The day he arrived, though, Mother Nature had other plans for us. I started my fucking period.

I was determined this wouldn't ruin our time together, but it did mean that the fucking was off the agenda. Oh, well. We had an equally awesome time making fun TikToks and touring cool spots downtown, including the ballparks, Campus Martius, and the Riverwalk. I'd even posted some photos of us to Facebook, which racked up the rather predictable Damn, who's the beefcake? or Woof! comments from my friends.

They weren't wrong. Alex was, undeniably, up there with the hottest guys I'd ever had the pleasure of banging.

Later that week, we drove out to Kelly's house to hang out with my family. Everyone instantly loved Alex, and the whole gang hounded me with comments and questions like, "Oh my gosh, Ty, he's great!" and "Why aren't you dating him?" Truth was, I just didn't feel like getting involved with a guy who lived so far away and was so much younger, and I hadn't had much time to really be myself after getting divorced. Right now, I was all about the fun. I was planning a trip to Tulum and Key West with my girls that summer – and, honestly, didn't think Alex was looking for a serious relationship, either.

The inability to be intimate didn't keep us from cuddling up on the couch back at my studio and watching TV and movies. We both fell asleep right there for the entire night. The next day, we drove an hour to stay the night at a lake house owned by my friends, James and Kelly, drinking on their boat, swimming, and sharing stories around the campfire.

***

Alex flew back to Dallas after the weekend, and I was left wondering what was wrong with me. This guy was fucking *perfect*. My friends and family all adored him, so why didn't I? Why wasn't I interested in more than just the sex? Perhaps it was because Alex had nothing about him that needed to be "fixed", and I wasn't ready for someone who wasn't a project.

I had a serious think about it and had another BAC.

Belief: If there's no work to be done in a relationship, then there's nothing in it that will validate you. You need there to be something to fix so you feel accomplished.

Action: You dismiss all of the good guys who would actually treat you right.

Challenge: You need to work on loving yourself first and foremost, so you are ready when a good man comes along. There won't be work to do because you already did the work — *on yourself.*

I chewed over this vicious cycle of mine for the next few weeks. My relationship history looked like a weather map of an incoming hurricane, with tornadoes circling around it in bright red cells. Time after time, I ignored the alerts to take shelter, instead walking right through the storms.

Fuck that. It was time – *way past* time – to make a change. I needed to spend some quality time by myself, blogging, pouring my feelings out in my art, and reading books on healing and practicing self-love.

The Fuckery that is...

A Kiss in the Rain.

"Beware of a wolf in sheep's clothing." – Aesop

I always went to at least one Carolina Panthers football game every year, and I worried that the pandemic was going to keep me from honoring my tradition. Imagine my excitement when my favorite NFL team opened their stadium again in late October!

Having seen on Facebook that Blake was still single, I asked him if he wanted to join me in Charlotte for the upcoming game. We'd stayed in touch enough for me to feel comfortable to offer him to stay in my hotel room, too. I'm not gonna lie – I was totally planning on banging him that night. Why not? I hadn't had sex in a long time, he was hot, and we were both single. What could it really turn into, anyway?

***

We both arrived at the hotel and got ready to go out for dinner and drinks before the game.

"Damn, you can see my balls in these!" Blake exclaimed as he pulled his pants on.

Me being me, I burst into a fit of giggles. It seemed he had a talent for hilarious one-liners – and sliding comments about his sizeable balls into our conversation every chance he got. When we sat down at the restaurant, he complained, under his breath, that the damn things were in the way.

Of course, I couldn't resist jumping on the sex-joke bandwagon, ordering my burger with ketchup, mayonnaise, and mustard – "The wetter, the better!"

The whole night was filled with comments like that – little not-quite-PG remarks that would become our inside jokes. I hadn't laughed so hard in so long, and it only got better during the game, as we downed beers and cracked jokes left and right.

***

The raindrops started to fall as the thermostat hit a balmy sixty-five degrees. We might have been in end-zone seats, but that did fuck all to protect my newly straightened hair.

Why do I even bother? I thought, throwing it into a messy bun on top of my head.

Blake, however, apparently didn't care about the drizzle. Or my fucked-up hair, judging by the way he was looking at me.

If the kiss that followed was anything to go by, he couldn't have given less of a shit. It was a heated one, the kind that sends shivers down your spine; and I knew in that moment, sitting in our little bubble six feet away from anyone else, that this wasn't going to be just a one-night fling.

The Fuckery that is...

Fools Rush In.

"Loving you was like going to war; I never came back the same"
– Warsan Shire

After our first night together, which concluded with club-hopping and romping, Blake and I were soon planning our next meetup. I decided to fly to see him a couple weeks later; and on that trip, we became exclusive.

Two weeks after that, while staying with me in Detroit for Thanksgiving, he told me he loved me.

Everyone I introduced him to thought he was wonderful. We spent the first two months falling ever deeper in love over FaceTime and alternating weekend visits. It really was like a fairy tale – no disagreements, no dishonesty, no red flags – and I was all in. How could I not be, when everything seemed so perfect?

***

My lease was up at the end of December. I knew things were moving fast with Blake and I, but I was feeling like maybe he could be "the one". Plus, Michigan's COVID restrictions, which still mandated quarantine, had me so depressed and lonely that moving out of state felt like the only way to preserve my well-being and sanity.

With this in mind, I went to meet Blake's family the week leading up to Christmas. They seemed to be a loving bunch, and I got along great with his mom, stepdad, and brother.

But there was something weird about Blake's mom. I'd seen them touching each other, rubbing each other's legs and shoulders, in a way that seemed unusual for a mother-and-son relationship. I even snuck away to call Shelly, whose own son was almost twenty, and asked her opinion. Perhaps I just hadn't grown up in a family that showed that kind of affection?

Her exact response was, "Uh, fuck no! That is *not* normal!"

So, I called Blake out on it. He told me they were just close; that after everything he'd put her through when he was younger, he'd learned to really appreciate his mom and always wanted to show her how much he loved her. I guess…? I mean, I don't know. My childhood was so fucked-up, there was no telling what I'd consider "normal".

***

I took the plunge, determined to move south as the New Year approached. The night before we were due to make the 12-hour long drive from Detroit, in a rented U-Haul full of my stuff, I invited some of my close friends to come over for one last small gathering. We did the usual, chatting, playing games, sipping beers; and by the end of it all, I was pretty beat. Never mind that

I'd spent most of the day packing and loading!

It stands to reason, then, that I just didn't feel like having sex. We'd already had sex a few times the day before, too, which had really drained my desire and energy. I told Blake this – and straight-up said "no" – several times when he tried to sleep with me; but, somehow, he coerced me into it.

What the fuck? I shouldn't feel uncomfortable around the guy I was all prepared to move across the country to be with, and he sure as *hell* shouldn't push me into being intimate with him! I started to question if I was making a huge mistake.

But I'd already committed – to Blake and to a relocation. *He wasn't a bad guy*, I thought to myself. Surely, this was just an isolated incident.

***

I settled into an apartment on the north side of the city. Even though we weren't yet living together, my place quickly became where we stayed; so, Blake invited his brother and his sister-in-law, Brandy, to come over for the evening.

After a couple hours, Brandy and I stepped outside. I decided to raise some concerns I had about Blake's ex-fiancée, Breanna. He claimed they'd split up after a disagreement over buying a house, and her selfishness about spending time with each other's families, but I had my doubts.

"That's not all of it," Brandy cautioned. "You'll have to ask him for the whole truth."

I did, right after they left. Blake revealed he'd been convicted of aggravated assault against Breanna.

"But she made it all up. She had a history of accusing guys of hurting her, you know," he insisted.

Now, these were some serious allegations. Blake said he had evidence of Breanna's manipulative behavior, and that photos taken on the night of the alleged incident would prove he hadn't touched her. I noticed some marks on Breanna in the pictures, which he assured me were just moles or other natural features of her skin.

I didn't know what to think. I took a massive step back from the relationship, and Blake could tell. He begged and pleaded with me to believe him, but all I saw was a man using these insecurities to make me feel like he'd been the victim all along.

Here we were, not even three months in, and I was no longer sure if he was the person he'd shown me he was in the beginning. But I didn't know anyone there in this new city, except Blake and his family (barely), so I decided to give him the benefit of the doubt. I would stay with him – for now.

The Fuckery that is...

Rage.

"Me, I'm dishonest, and you can always trust a dishonest man to be dishonest. Honestly, it's the honest ones you have to watch out for." – Johnny Depp

One night in mid-January, Blake and I met up with his brother and cousins for a sort of "triple date". I went outside with the girls for a short while, chatting it up, when, out of nowhere, I got an angry text message from Blake. He called me inconsiderate and threatened to leave me there. What the hell? I was just talking to his relatives. It wasn't like I'd taken one of the guys out there and tried to get in their pants!

I caught up with him at the bar, where he spent a solid few minutes yelling at me.

"There are plenty of other girls in here!" he shouted, shoving his hand in my face before stalking off. He didn't outright hit me, but his palm did brush my nose.

That was my first taste of his aggression.

***

Over the next couple of weeks, our fights were insane. When I caught Blake going through my MacBook, and he lied about it, the ensuing argument turned into a two-day fiasco where he called me names and screamed at me. He was adamant that he was telling the truth, that he'd done nothing wrong; but I knew what I saw, so I pulled the system records from that morning and caught him red-handed. The only way that *wasn't* him was if someone broke into my place – while he was there! – took the time to scroll through my browser history and Facebook posts and left without making a sound.

He finally admitted it, in case you're wondering.

Another particularly memorable instance of his fuckery happened while we were visiting a restaurant. I'd stepped out to the patio, where an older gentleman struck up a polite conversation with me. When we left, Blake demanded to know if I'd gotten the man's number. He was storming, furious, accusing me of nonsense.

It was at that same spot, a couple weeks later, that everyone there saw him grab my arm, curse at me, and pull me behind him back to the car.

***

February 6th. Kristin and Jamie, two of my good friends from Detroit who I'd played sports with for years, flew down for the weekend. Kristin and I were in my bathroom, doing our makeup and getting ready for a fun night out, while Blake was in the next room, eavesdropping (this wasn't so unusual – I'd caught him listening in on my phone conversations several times.).

When I came out, Blake asked me what we'd been discussing. He was adamant I'd been talking shit about him, had said something like, "He has no idea". To this day, I don't know what I said, or what he thought he heard – and damn, I didn't realize an insignificant chat with one of my girlfriends was enough reason to put me on trial!

So, in the Uber on our way home, I asked Kristin if she recalled me saying that to her. Blake, who was sitting in the front seat, blew my phone up with nasty text messages. Evidently, my attempt to get an honest answer for him enraged him.

***

As soon as we got back, Blake dragged me into the bathroom and berated me, pushing his face so heavily to mine I could feel his breath. I didn't manage to get a word in before his hand was in my face, his palm against my nose, and he shoved me with such force my eyes began to water.

Trying to stay calm, to get past him and escape, I told him to get away from me. He didn't listen. He grabbed the can of beer he'd only just taken the top off, held it in front of me, and crushed it, sending a jet of stinging liquid right into my eyes. The explosion was so intense, it splattered all over the counter, floor, mirror, and a framed photo of a crooked dock, one that I'd taken, hanging on the wall next to me.

I stumbled out of the bathroom, completely drenched in beer, tears streaming down my cheeks from a combination of him shoving me and my uncontrollable crying. My friends immediately rallied round me, after all they had heard us arguing from just one room over.

"Get the fuck out!" I shrieked the moment Blake dared to show himself.

Of course, he refused, and my friend Jamie had to take him outside for almost an hour to get him to accept it. Blake kept saying he was sorry, that he didn't mean it, that he loved me and didn't want to go, but we all knew it was bullshit.

Not even an hour later, he texted me.

I'm sorry things escalated the way they did tonight. I didn't mean to touch you like that, at all. I'll reconvene tomorrow. Enjoy your night with them.

Two hours later, at 1:37 AM, another text.

My stomach is in knots. This doesn't feel right WTF... I hate this. I hate myself right now. For all the insecurities and imperfections. Knowing I love you with my everything. I can't lose you. I'm so sorry for everything.

I knew I *had* to get out of this relationship, but how could I do it without angering him more? He'd even threatened, to me and his family, to commit suicide if I left him...

***

Blake eventually agreed to get help, go to therapy, and work on himself. I wanted him to – I wanted him to be that good guy he'd pretended to be. I even sent him articles about how to stop being abusive to your partner, which he thanked me for.

But I knew deep down that, much like my dream vision of John, the guy I was with wasn't real.

I also had a few text conversations with Brandy. It turned out Blake admitted everything to her, except he'd told her the absolute lie that he was trying to walk away from me when he put his hand up, and I "ran into" his hand with my nose.

I had a BAC.

Belief: This is a dangerous person. You need to be very careful how you proceed. Remember when you were a kid, what your stepdad put you and your family through? Every time you guys tried to leave, he would threaten to hurt you.

Action: Do your best to keep things amicable until you have a solid exit strategy.

Challenge: This is a dangerous person. Do not proceed. Get out now, even if it means leaving everything behind. Pack your car, get Bula, and *go*. Nothing you own is as important as your life or your body. No lease or contract is worth trying to salvage.

The Fuckery that is...

Getting Out.

"No one can make you feel inferior without your consent." –
Eleanor Roosevelt

Blake was generally calmer over the next month; but I was still
secretly planning to get away from him. Shitty things still
happened: he'd hide my phone from me during fights, and one
day, he sat outside my apartment in his car, watching my every
move, for six whole hours. When I spotted him and sent him a
message, asking what he was doing, he claimed he was at work.

***

On a weekend in early March, I took a flight to Dallas. I need some
time with my best friend, Shelly, and the other girls who I missed
so much.

While I was gone, Blake discovered the security camera that sat,
out in the open, on my work desk.

"When did you put that up?" he asked as we talked on the phone,
separated by multiple state lines.

"What do you mean? I've always had that camera."

It *was* the exact same device I'd owned for years. Why was he acting like it was bizarre that I had it? It's not like having an in-home camera, especially in my workspace where I kept a lot of valuable items, was unusual. I liked the comfort of knowing it was there in case someone ever broke in, and I'd use it to keep an eye on Bula when I was away, sometimes.

His continued line of questioning had me curious, so I opened up the camera app and took a look at some of the footage. It was so fucking disturbing. His behavior was, quite frankly, psychotic. He would walk up to it, staring into it, saying shit like, "Oh, you see me?" or, "I see you. I see you just turned it on." He was even talking to the dogs: "Mommy's got a camera, she's watching us. Say hello to Momma. Look, she's got a camera, say hi!"

At one point, he kept going up to a picture frame sitting on the light stand, picking it up and laying it down flat. What was his obsession with it? I had to listen closely to catch his words.

"Mommy had someone over here, didn't she? Who was here, puppies? We're gonna have to have a talk about that."

What in the actual fuck? How could I have asked someone over? I didn't know anyone in the entire city other than him and his family. He'd officially proven to me that he was off his rocker, but I didn't let on to Blake that I knew about this odd behavior.

***

When I was in Dallas, I decided I'd try to move back there, to be closer to the friends I'd made in the year I lived there with John. I lined up a couple of interviews, and even looked at a few apartments.

I had to travel there again for a funeral around a fortnight later, which, although sad, ended up having great timing, since I was able to interview with the same mobile company I had a contract with the year before while I was there. You know, the same company Blake worked for.

I was doing everything in my power to string Blake along without so much of a hint that I was planning to leave him. But when I got the job offer, I knew I had to tell him. If I waited, there was every chance he'd find out some other way and go off on me.

So, I called Blake to let him know, and he acted happy for me. He did begin to question me about "us", but I assured him this would be good for our relationship in the long-term. What I really meant was this was best for *me*, but I had to pretend to him like *we* would be okay until I could actually leave.

"Let me take this career victory," I said, playing it off, "move in and get settled, and it'll all work out down the line."

***

I'd just gotten back to Shelly's, and she encouraged me to check my camera app, mostly because she'd overheard my conversation with Blake. I am so glad I did. He'd completely lost his shit as soon as we got off the phone, ranting to himself about me being a selfish bitch, a narcissist, inconsiderate, disrespectful, and making other outlandish comments. He even got the dogs involved.

"Mommy's an inconsiderate bitch! She didn't say *we* are moving to Dallas, she said *I* am moving to Dallas. She doesn't even think about *me*. We're in a relationship, we're trying to have a future together, but she says *I* am moving to Dallas, not *we* are moving to Dallas."

No, I wasn't thinking about him, or even us. I was thinking about me, my safety, and my future. This was my career choice, mine alone, and it was my way out.

Shelly urged me to save the footage in case Blake did something truly insane and I'd need to use it in my defense. Not even 10 minutes later, I found out he'd called the corporate office and asked to be relocated… to Dallas.

***

What's even creepier than that, you ask? When he called me, he was being all sweet to me, telling me he loved me and was excited for me, and followed it up with this text. Yes, one letter at a time.

I
L
O
V
E
Y
O
U

I was just boarding my flight back at the time, and was talking to the person sitting next to me. When I didn't reply right away, Blake angrily messaged me back-to-back, asking if I got his text(s) and demanding I tell him I loved him too.

***

The next day, I called him out on everything I'd seen on the camera footage. He claimed he was just upset, and he didn't mean any of it, but I had zero fucks left to give to this asshole. I broke up with him and told him he had three days to get his shit out of my place.

For fear he'd turn into the monster I knew he was inside, I kept things as amicable as possible while I packed up to move to Dallas. Fortunately, Blake kept his cool, and we even met up for dinner and drinks before I left, agreeing to stay friends after the fact.

I always want to believe that there's good in people. I, myself, was once a young and insecure girl who got paranoid over stupid shit; so, a small part of me still hoped he'd work on himself and change.

Oh, how wrong I was.

The Fuckery that is...

Dallas.

"Of all the things my hands have touched, the best is my paintbrush, the worst is you." – *Ty Paige*

I was out running, training for a 5K, when I got a call from Blake.

"Guess what? I got the job transfer! I'm coming to Dallas."

I told him multiple times, "Do *not* move to Dallas for me!". Yet he insisted that he'd always wanted to live in Dallas, and that he had friends and family there, too.

I was unbelievably uncomfortable. I knew we had no chance of a future together; but my fear was confused by my hope that eventually, he'd be different.

***

He'd relocated by the end of April. We hung out a few times at the two usual places I frequented, Chill Bar (where I would hang out when I lived in Dallas the year before), and Hebron Station in Lewisville. I even introduced him to a handful of my friends, a couple of whom warned me to be careful, because they knew about Blake's violent tendencies.

He hadn't shown any signs of aggression in a while, and even told me he was still in therapy every week. He tried to claim he was "a new man", but I thought, shit honey I've been seeing counselors for over thirty years and still acknowledge I needed to keep working on myself. So, I never once believed he was "healed". I reminded him of that every time he tried to convince me he'd "changed". It takes years, Blake – not a couple months.

***

Saturday, May 15th. We'd gone to Chill for brunch, then to Hebron to play volleyball. Blake's eyes had held anger all day. I asked him several times if we should go separate ways, since he seemed like he was in a bad mood. He was determined we'd be together all that day and night.

The mean, degrading comments under his breath, the verbal stabs at me for talking to people who weren't him… There was no mistaking it. The monster was coming. I could see it in his face, feel it in my bones.

9:36 PM. I called Shelly while he was in the gas station.

"I feel like I'm in danger. I *know* something bad's about to happen."

"Don't worry, Ty. I'll keep my phone on, *no matter what*," she assured me.

I hung up as soon as I saw Blake walk out, then deleted the call from my log.

We got back to my place, and I said I wanted to stay in. If he didn't like that, he could go home. He countered by suggesting a restaurant nearby. Food sounded good, and at least if we were in public, he couldn't do anything. Right?

Right?

At the bar, Blake was talking sports with a few guys next to us. When he left to go to the bathroom, I chatted with them, too. I tried to tell one of them that I was nervous about Blake's temper, but he emerged right as I finished saying it. I had to whisper and motion a quick "shh" to the guy.

Blake caught me.

He made a huge scene, demanding that we tell him what was going on; calling us liars, insinuating that we were flirting with each other. Neither me nor the guys could calm him down, and I made a quick exit, wanting to get away from this shit as fast as possible. I tossed my purse into my car, shut the door, and locked it.

"Get an Uber," I said bluntly when Blake approached me.

"No."

"Get an Uber home, Blake."

"No."

We arrived at my apartment for the second time that night. I couldn't find my phone, and Blake was still screaming at me about the "shh" incident.

"It was nothing!" I told him, over and over again. "Do you honestly think I'd flirt with another guy while you're there?"

He followed me up the stairs, into my living space, shouting hateful, harmful words at me for over an hour. The only defense I had was to keep demanding that he get the fuck out.

But he wouldn't. He would not leave.

Amidst his rage, Blake stomped over to my security camera – which I'd set up in my new place, just as I had everywhere I'd lived in the last few years – and ripped it out the wall socket. He went out on to my balcony and used his baseball-pitcher arm strength to throw it as far as he could.

Oh, fuck. I was so scared I could barely think. I'd told him to leave more times than I could count.

He lurched into the hallway, towards the display case where I kept the glass awards my agency had won. Each one was heavy, with a spear-shaped point. He seized one of them and rounded on me.

"You have to keep these on display to remind yourself, because you're a piece of shit!" he shouted.

Was he going to throw it at me? Hit me with it? Thank God, no. He launched my keys and his watch at me, instead, which shattered my key fob into pieces that scattered under the bed and over the window frame.

I retreated to the living room, trying once again to get him to leave, and just like that – what I'd known was going to happen, all day long, happened.

I was standing next to the eat-in kitchen counter, which was perpendicular to my couch in the living room. Blake, with his 200-pound, six-foot-three frame and nearly black eyes, came out from the hallway between the kitchen and bedroom, and clamped his hand over my entire face to shut me up. He then pressed his cheek to mine, bellowing right in my ear.

"Blake, back up. Please."

Blake withdrew his hands, then thrust them both at my shoulders with all his force. I hit the wooden frame of my couch so hard that it made an audible sound, and then my body met the floor. I cried out in pain, yelling that he'd hurt me, I couldn't move, he'd ruined my chances of running the 5K.

"Get the fuck out!" I screamed at the top of my lungs.

He immediately apologized, begging me not to call the police as he scrambled to gather his stuff and, finally, *leave*.

4:15 AM. My downstairs neighbor was sitting outside and watched Blake go. As I'd soon find out, she'd heard everything.

A few minutes after he finally left, I stood up. I was in excruciating pain. I still couldn't find my phone, so I grabbed my MacBook and called my four closest friends who lived nearby. One of them answered but couldn't make out what I was saying. When Shelly picked up, she knew exactly what was going on, and came over immediately, quickly followed by Christy.

When I'd calmed down some, I opened the Find my iPhone MacBook app to locate my phone, which was lodged between the seat and console of my car. I already knew Blake had hidden it from me, but when I asked him, he said he didn't know where it was. He tried to tell me he saw it in my bedroom, along with my purse – total bullshit, since neither had been in there. I also mentioned my security camera. He said he definitely had no idea where it was, and claimed he never touched it.

As for the knot on my back, it kept getting bigger over the next few hours, eventually settling as a bruised lump the size of a softball. It hurt so bad I could barely even sit, let alone drive, and took nearly three weeks to heal fully. I made sure to take photos of it every single day.

The Fuckery that is...

A Psychopath.

"Psychopaths view any social exchange as a 'feeding opportunity' – a contest or a test of wills in which there can only be one winner. Their motives are to manipulate and take, ruthlessly and without remorse." – Robert D. Hare

Blake had the audacity to text me later that day, asking me to mail him his watch and some clothes he'd left behind. Oh, the watch you *threw* at me? I don't fucking think so. I had one goal in my communication with him: to make him to admit to throwing my security camera off my balcony. Luckily, he did, right before I told him to never contact me again.

But, if you know anything about obsession, it doesn't just end like that. In true psychopath fashion, he began a campaign of lying, manipulation, stalking, and harassment.

I ignored every text Blake sent me from then on. I stayed home, refusing to go anywhere for almost a week because I was so distraught and hurt. Rumors began circulating through my social circle that he'd been hanging out at Chill and Hebron all the fucking time, starting on the day he assaulted me.

He'd only lived in Dallas for about two weeks, while I'd been a resident before, and my friends and I were known regulars at both venues. Besides, remember? – He didn't move to Dallas for me – he said he had folks here! Why the hell was he going to these places – places that were a good 25-minute drive from where he lived?

To add to this bullshit, people I knew told me about the lies Blake was spouting to anyone who would listen:

"Oh, she just fell."

"Well, maybe I blacked out."

"I don't remember, I blacked out!"

"I didn't *hit* her." (Almost sounding like an admission that he did *something*, just not direct assault.)

"She left her phone in the car." (And how did he know where it was, considering I never told him where I found it?)

I caved, sending him a text that politely asked him to leave me and my friends alone.

How could I have let this happen? I thought. *I'm so much smarter than that. I love myself more than that.* Did I really believe that we could be friends, that he would change, after the way he'd treated me back in my apartment? My God, he already had a felony conviction for this exact same thing!

I felt so ashamed, and my musings prompted a BAC.

***

Four days later, Blake texted me again. He missed me, he was sorry, he hoped we could be friends one day. I ignored it. I had a hunch that he was planning something, and I created a free profile on a popular dating app to test it. I wasn't interested in dating; but I knew that with his obsessive, possessive, insecure tendencies, Blake would do everything he could to find me on there. If he contacted me, it'd give serious sustenance to the case I'd started building against him.

Within hours of adding a few pics and a brief intro, he sent me a screenshot of my profile, along with a nasty comment that had every other letter capitalized. I had to Google what that formatting meant, and it turned out to be some immature form of mockery. *Ugh.*

Not 12 hours later, I received a message on the dating app from a six-foot-four, athletic guy with a perfectly symmetrical face and bit of sexy stubble. His name was – you guessed it – *Blake*. Blake

Fallon, to be exact. He appeared to be everything I wanted in a man: 42 years old, lived just a mile from me, did not want kids, and a diehard Panthers fan.

Shame it was too good to be true, *Blake*. Did you even try to fool me?

I swear, this man must have thought I had less than the average number of brain cells. But I entertained "Mr. Fallon" for a few hours. He asked what my plans were for that evening, and I said I was meeting a friend for dinner. Of course, he followed up by inviting me to hang out afterwards, even giving me a phone number to text him on.

After a brief investigation, I matched this number with that of a guy I actually knew. That was all the evidence I needed, and I cut off communication.

I hadn't really planned to check the message thread again, but I'm glad I did.

He'd sent me a different number, with an apology that the first one he'd provided was wrong. Creepy. As. Fuck, and painfully obvious that he was impersonating someone else to deceive and stalk me, trying to pin down precisely where I'd be that night. Enough was enough.

I replied with the acronym WUDNTBE, which stood for "what's understood doesn't need to be explained" – one of our previous inside jokes.

His reply?

Haha, this was fun while it lasted! Hope we can be friends soon.

Not fucking funny, Blake.

This is stalking, harassment and psychotic behavior, I messaged him back immediately.

On top of the physical abuse you already caused, this is mental abuse. I am calling the police.

The fake profile was gone within minutes. Did you know it's a crime to impersonate someone online with the intent to deceive another person?

That night, as soon as I got home, I did exactly what I said I would and filed a report with the cops. I pressed charges for aggravated assault, domestic violence; and, when the officer suggested I get a protection order, as well as formally report the first incident that happened a couple months prior, I followed their advice there and then.

The Fuckery that is...

Harassment.

"I have lived in hell, and I have lived in Heaven, and I can tell you – I'm most comfortable somewhere in between, because it feels the most real." – Ty Paige

Over the next five months, I did everything the detective assigned to my case told me to do. I had to constantly watch my back, keeping note of every incident, each date, time, and place. I barely left my home. I hated feeling like a prisoner in my apartment complex, so I made a habit of going to my pool every day as soon as I was done with work. At least it helped relieve a little of the stress.

Speaking of work, the company that employed us both had been informed about Blake's actions – but, perhaps predictably, they didn't do anything. When I eventually resigned, out of fear that I'd encounter Blake if I went into the office, they made me sign a contract saying I released them from any liability. Way to show you give a shit, corporate America! If – or when – the day comes that this guy kills a woman, I hope they remember they had the chance to take a moral stand against him, but didn't.

***

Before I blocked Blake on social media, I found he'd made several posts about me. He, stupidly, put out indirect, or even direct, jabs; commented on them, edited them, deleted them. My God, the level of paranoia this guy suffered from was so high. He kept trying to add my friends on Facebook, all while I was removing anyone remotely associated with him from my own profile. He has even had a few of his buddies try to add me; and he even posted publicly that he'd reached out to John to try and get dirt on me!

If that wasn't enough bullshit, Blake was still staking out Chill Bar every single night, racking up $200 tabs buying shots and drinks for people he thought were somehow tied to me. The managers and employees, who knew me – and I'd explained my situation pretty well – didn't seem to spare much thought for my safety – they'd even befriended Blake!

I'd already stopped going there; and, honestly, the whole mess made me realize just how crappy that joint was. Never once did I aspire to be tagged in Facebook posts by a fucking bar in Texas. It used to be a cool spot for my girlfriends and I to grab happy hour drinks, but all in all, I was quite happy not to be associated with that place anymore. Fuck that, Blake could have it!

Over the course of the next few months, his harassment continued, taking ever-more-insidious forms. He used my toll tag illegally and bragged about it; watched me from afar; had friends spy on and videotape me; tried to befriend anyone I knew; dated any girl he could within my social circle (using them to try and get to me, of course).

He even avoided arrest by warrant by borrowing a car from one of those girls. The online stalking never stopped, reaching its peak when he hacked into my streaming accounts, creating multiple profiles, seeking to keep himself lodged in my psyche.

***

In mid-June, I decided it was time to get the full truth from Blake's ex-fiancée, Breanna. I sent her a message on Facebook, and within minutes, she responded.

Oh my God, call me.

My stomach wrapped itself into knots as I dialed the number she'd provided. They tightened, squeezing so hard I thought I might throw up, as I made the call, and the phone rang.

I was about to talk to the woman who he'd accused of manipulating him, lying about him – a reality I'd now lived myself. I wanted to hear it from her. I had to know, to be absolutely certain that what she'd accused him of really did happen.

"Hey, girl!" she greeted, as if we'd known each other for years.

Breanna and I talked for over two hours; and hearing what she went through, I realized how lucky I was to have escaped Blake when I did, that I didn't dismiss his abuse. Her experiences were utterly terrifying. He'd tracked her phone, punched her, bit her, choked her, raped her, held a fucking gun to her head. But I understood why she'd stayed with him for two years: like me, she believed he could change. She felt bad for him, and she wanted that Lifetime-movie love story ending, where the guy makes a total 180 into the man of her dreams.

It didn't take long for us to develop a friendship. The week Blake signed the protection order, Breanna and I met in person while she was on a layover in Dallas; and she revealed possibly the creepiest thing yet about her ordeal with Blake. Sometimes, his mom would come over to her house to intervene their fights. She'd physically restrain him, which made enough sense; but then she'd start stroking his face, saying things like, "Come back to me, baby boy, Jesus is with you."

Ugh. I shuddered just typing that. I suppose it went some way to explaining all the weird touchy-feely stuff I'd witnessed between them. Then again, I couldn't really blame her for thinking her son was possessed – the way his eyes would literally change color when he was enraged, like you see in horror movies, was enough to put that thought into anyone's mind.

I hated the eyes I'd seen in his police mugshot. They didn't even look real.

***

There was no way I was ever going to feel safe, living 30 minutes from Blake and having to deal with him stalking me and spreading lies and rumors anywhere I went. Even in the supposed sanctuary my own home, I'd open a streaming service and see yet another profile he'd hacked in and created under his name.

I couldn't let him control my life any further. I had to start living for myself, again – and this time, *really* commit to it. So, I landed a sweet job as a director at an advertising agency in South Florida and got the fuck out.

As I soared into the clouds towards another fresh start, I had pretty disturbing BAC.

Belief: So many of the people you know here believe his lies, which makes *you* look like the liar.

Action: You feel so bad for the new girl he is dating; she has no idea what she's in for. You should try to warn her, just in case she doesn't know about his prior felony and the new charges.

Challenge: Let karma play out the way it's supposed to. It's not your fault, and you can't control his, or her, destiny. All those people see what you initially saw: a good-looking, charming guy. But a truly good person doesn't have to try so hard to look like one. The truth will reveal itself eventually.

The Fuckery that is...

Being Single on Purpose.

"I'm happy. Not because everything is perfect, but because everything is not perfect, and I am doing just fine." – Ty Paige

Finally, I started to realize that my world could be anything I wanted it to be. *I* could make it that way. I made the decision to be alone, *really* alone, for as long as possible – to stay single on purpose, not even desiring to be in a relationship. No dating, no flings, no men, full stop. To be honest, I didn't *want* to be touched; it was difficult to fathom the thought after what I'd been through with Blake.

I knew it was going to be hard. I've always been a people person; and, until the incident in my Dallas apartment, I'd always enjoyed romantic (and sexual) companionship. But I'd moved to a new city, in a new state, and was about to take on an entirely new life.

There was no better time to focus on my career, my own happiness – just *me*. I even bought myself a gorgeous peridot-and-diamond ring set in rose gold. As I placed it onto my ring finger, I made myself a promise – much like a proposal to myself – and jotted down a list of everything I'd do along my self-love journey.

***

Shelly and I drove across the country together to get me all settled into my new home. As we ventured from Dallas to Fort Lauderdale, it hit me. I was embarking on a journey that I could truly call my own – and starting over at my age didn't have to be terrifying.

Eighteen hours later, after a drive-through margarita stop in New Orleans, overnighting in the Florida panhandle, and a couple of horrific, torrential downpours that had me shaking harder than any orgasm I've ever had, we arrived.

I'd always said I'd never live in Florida. I'm a Midwest girl, for fuck's sake! I love fall – all the seasons, really, including winter. There's something so calming and peaceful about watching the snow fall outside; and going for walks in the flurries, all wrapped up like the kid in *A Christmas Story*, is utterly magical. But I'd had to seize the opportunity I'd been offered, not just because those directorial posts weren't exactly a dime a dozen…

Who knows, I thought, *perhaps I'll break down even more of my beliefs in the Sunshine State.*

***

Since I'd already started working for the agency remotely, I knew my team pretty well, and that we'd be taking on a lot in the first four weeks I was on the ground with them. With my own business having been reduced to life support and, after 13 years in operation, finally dying a "ripcord" death during the pandemic, it was beyond-words-amazing to be busy again. Contributing my creative talents to huge, meaningful projects made me feel like I had a purpose; and work was the only thing I wanted to focus on.

As I got into the swing of the next stage of my life, I created a simple BAC to help me along.

Belief: You can't be happy without a romantic partner.

Action: You're always looking, even when you say you're not. You're peeking around every corner, hoping that Mr. Right is standing there, ready to walk straight up to you and sweep you off your feet. You go out, even by yourself, with the secret hope that you'll meet someone.

Challenge: Be your own partner! Date yourself loyally, and do not look anywhere for *anyone*. Say no to any guy who asks you out or shows interest. You're in a relationship with yourself right now, and you don't cheat. Period.

***

As it turned out, Fort Lauderdale was the perfect place to focus on being single on purpose. I mean, how the fuck was I supposed to keep up with the hottie-totty twenty-somethings running around in their whopping size-zero thong bikinis? I was happy with the way I looked, don't get me wrong; and really, I had absolutely no interest in trying to compete with those Miami-type model figures. The thought alone was exhausting, and it just solidified my exclusivity with myself.

The first month of "Project Single on Purpose" was tough, as I'd expected. I didn't have any friends in the area except a woman named Ilene, who I'd met on one of my first nights in the city

while visiting a brewery with Shelly
.

We instantly connected and exchanged phone numbers. Ilene had recently lost her husband of over 25 years; and, since she had two young adult sons at home, I knew she wasn't going to be someone I could call on any time I wanted to get out and do something. Still, it was comforting to have a new girlfriend that was hip, fun, and down-to-earth, much like me.

I spent my time working, relaxing at home, taking Bula for walks, and waking up early to go watch the sunrise at the nearby beach (an activity that soon became a once-, or even twice-weekly, ritual). It was an ideal spot to meditate and reflect, with the light of a brand-new day shining on my face; and, when the clouds covered the sun, it created the perfect contrast for pictures! I spent many a happy mornings there, snapping away with my iPhone, and posting the results to my Instagram account.

***

I was discovering what it really meant to date myself, too. Solo visits to restaurants or bars became my new normal, and I started cooking for myself as much as I could, enjoying dinner at home all alone. I'd even make myself breakfast in bed, sometimes for dinner! I also ordered a daunting, 1,000-piece, *Friends*-themed puzzle, designed entirely in the show's iconic black-and-white-type font. In just three weeks and about 25 hours, I'd completed that fucker – all by myself.

Not wanting to limit myself to indoor pursuits and city life, I took the plunge (haha!) and joined a paddle boarding group on Facebook. Although it was fall, the temperatures stayed in the high 80s or even 90s some days, so I wanted to take advantage of the extended summer, something I'd never experienced in Michigan. After exchanging some comments with her, I became Facebook friends with a girl named Beth, a fellow stand-up paddle boarding enthusiast who lived about 20 minutes north of me. We even, ironically, had a mutual friend we'd both played volleyball with back in Michigan!

We made plans to meet up for a cruise down the canal; but first, I had to make sure my board was ready. I'd sold my standard board a year before (there weren't many spots to take it to in uber-urban Detroit), and I didn't have room for a full-sized one in my new place. Luckily, Amazon came to the rescue, delivering a shiny, new blow-up one right to my doorstep.

My first attempt to launch the thing was a major failure. I took it out to a local boarding spot, along with an electric pump I'd bought in my desperation to avoid using a manual one. I mean, what could be more unattractive than me standing on the beach, plunging my arms up and down for over ten minutes in the world's shittiest imitation of the chicken dance while turning beet-red from the effort? Or maybe I'm just fucking lazy. Either way, that automatic pump was my only option.

Anyway, I didn't bring the right nozzle for the damn thing, and after nearly an hour of trying to get the board to blow up all the way and it deflating every time, I gave up. It was a Saturday afternoon, I looked like death warmed up after sweating my ass off standing in the sun and the heat of my car's exhaust, and I had absolutely nothing to show for it.

I took a step back. Who the hell was I trying to impress, anyway? No one, I reminded myself. Only me. So, I popped into the brewery to cool off with an afternoon beer and had a BAC.

***

Shit, being single on purpose meant I had to do things I'd normally ask a guy to help with, or even do. But look at everything I'd done for myself, by myself, in the last month. Being alone didn't mean I was helpless, nor did it mean I was lonely. I was claiming my independence, and, for the first time in my life, loving my true self, not who I was when I was with someone, be that family, friends, or lovers.

I was starting to feel so comfortable in my own skin; but I realized maybe it was time to start being social again. I hadn't gone out much, mostly because I didn't want to cloud my own judgment if, by chance, some ridiculously good-looking guy with a hot British accent sat down next to me somewhere! Enough time had passed that I'd started feeling true love feelings for myself, to a point where I knew I'd stay faithful to my mission. It got me thinking: why are we so loyal to other people, but often not so to ourselves?

Here comes one fuckery of a BAC!

Belief: You're loyal to others, and they should be loyal to you.

Action: You're always there for everyone, are honest and truthful as often as possible, and faithful to your friends and partners. If you're not, you're betraying them. And there is nothing worse than betrayal.

Challenge: Be loyal to yourself for once, Ty. Don't cheat on yourself, just the same as you wouldn't cheat on a partner.

The Fuckery that is...

New People.

"I'll never stop being too good to people. It's who I am, and I love who I am. At the end of it all, I'll look back knowing I was the one who gave the most, cared the most and loved the most. If all I get in return is the loss of a friendship, it's really a gain. Because someone else who values me will happily take their place - and be grateful." – Ty Paige

Other than Ilene and Beth, I'd met a handful of new buddies by way of Vega Lounge, a little dive bar tucked inside a strip mall next to a well-known, "Tinder date" type of restaurant called Foundry. I'd first discovered this place after having brunch at Foundry, when I'd chatted with a few friendly tourists sitting at Vega's outside table, as well as a couple locals, over a drink and figured the vibe seemed pretty aligned with my preference for a low-key crowd.

The first friend I made there was an older gentleman named Paul, who had the friendliest voice and was always ready to tell you a story. I mentioned that I'd just moved to Fort Lauderdale and was still learning my way around, and he was quick to offer up advice on where to go and what to do. He adored cycling – something we didn't have in common – but his passion, when he recounted his adventures riding around South Florida, was infectious. I felt damn near ashamed when I admitted, with a laugh, "I don't even own a bicycle!"

We exchanged phone numbers, and Paul said he'd be happy to introduce me to some of the other regulars there, folks he knew well that were "good souls". I could tell immediately that Paul was a good old soul; so, of course, I agreed.

***

I encountered a few new faces just by stopping into Vega a couple times a week; and, refreshingly, I wasn't hit on by anyone. Not that such a thing's usual for me – I don't really get approached much, if ever – but the first-month fears that I'd fail to toe the line of being faithful to myself had taken a while to subside. Fortunately, they'd finally diminished. Even thinking about meeting someone wasn't a possibility in my mind anymore, being so far outweighed by my excitement about finally being true to myself and committing to my own happiness.

I hadn't formed what I'd consider a real *friendship* with anyone, though. Sure, I met people and learned their names; but Beth, Paul, and Ilene were the only people I'd even exchanged phone numbers with. Back in Detroit, if you met someone out somewhere, you typically invited them to join your social circle within a couple days. Midwest folks were just so different than the people I was meeting in Florida. Feeling like I was struggling to fit in, I had a little flashback-to-middle-school style BAC.

> **Belief:** If you don't have any friends you can be with often, you have little value.
>
> **Action:** Meet people anywhere you can and be likeable, so they want to be your friend.
>
> **Challenge:** Stop trying to please people all the time. If someone wants to be in your life, they will be. If they don't, they won't be. You cannot control this. You have a shitload of wonderful friends in your life. They may not physically be where you are, but the abundance of love and support you have from them is overwhelming. This may not be the place to make more lifelong friendships.

Yeah, that challenge was going to be a *very* hard pill for me to swallow. Having people around me all the time meant, in a way, that I could avoid having to get to know myself. This was the first time I'd spent any significant period all by myself and doing so forced me to like myself, to *love* myself. I hung out with the Vega gang on my own terms; I chose to leave alone, and never felt bad about it.

I was pretty sure, by now, I was figuring out who the real Ty was.

The Fuckery that is...

Cheating on Myself.

"To evolve, you just need L-O-V-E" – Ty Paige

It was a Saturday in mid-October, and I was moving full speed ahead in my relationship with myself. I'd treated myself to a little spa day at home, complete with a bubble bath, facial, nail session, and a glass of cold Pinot Grigio. I was feeling fucking pretty, so I put on a casual, cute outfit and took myself out for an evening meal.

A couple after-dinner drinks were definitely in order, so I stopped by a swanky bar in the high-end part of town. I had no intention of meeting anyone, or even really talking to anyone, which was pretty easy to do round there. The small tourist groups were, usually, made up of close friends who didn't invite outsiders in; and the locals were often stuffy or stuck-up, preferring to keep to their own little bubbles. I would, on occasion, have a random old man try to strike up conversation with me – for some weird reason, I tended to attract guys in their 60s – but it was easy enough to turn them down.

As I headed towards home, I decided to swing by Vega, because why the fuck not? I was, by now, on a first-name basis with the bartenders, who knew my order would always be the same: a bottle of beer-water. I sat down outside, nodding a quick hello to one of the guys – someone Paul had introduced me to – at the next table.

I could tell he'd been drinking a bit. He'd seemed pretty reserved the first time we'd met; but now, it seemed nothing could stop him talking. Before long, he invited me to join him and his buddy.

"Sure!" I grabbed my bottle and clutch and shuffled over. The table was a four-top, so I avoided having to sit awkwardly next to a couple of near-strangers.

"I'm Ty, nice to meet you!" I offered up an introduction to the other guy at the table.

"Garza. Nice meeting you, too!"

Oh, boy. I'd already noted that Garza was attractive, with his even, deep-brown skin, piercing eyes, and buff arms and shoulders, as if he could scoop you up and, effortlessly, whisk you away like a storybook princess. The recipe was perfect as-was – but, fuck, the moment he opened his mouth and I heard that dreamy Jamaican accent, it was like sprinkles on the icing on the cake!

***

We talked for over two hours, and then took a walk down to the beach. Sitting together, right on the edge of the water, I mentioned I hadn't really spent much time at the beach aside from my weekly sunrise meditations. In return, he told me all about his family.

He'd been divorced for just three years and had two daughters aged six and thirteen. I rattled off a little about my own relationship history, without going into all the gory details – determined to keep that criminal, Blake, in the past as much as possible.

I wasn't anticipating that anything would happen between us. Even if there was a mutual attraction, I'd resolved to treat my relationship with myself just as seriously as if I were with someone. I'd never had an issue with a casual conversation, with someone other than my partner, turning into anything physical. So why would I let it now that my S.O. was me?

Well, shit – it all went to crap as soon as Garza kissed me. I responded, more than willingly, and we shared a super indulgent few seconds that seemed to stretch on and on, forever, to a place where it was just us two. I felt that damn kiss reach into my soul and grab it by a thread – just a thread, because the moment we pulled apart, I felt so horribly guilty I could only hope that it broke before it stitched.

The next day, I had my BAC.

Belief: You cheated on yourself.

Action: You didn't hurt anyone else by doing this.

Challenge: You matter just as much as anyone else. Your feelings matter! You know how you felt when your exes cheated on you? This is the same. But you forgave them, so you have to forgive yourself. You don't have to forget – that's where the lesson is learned – but forgive yourself. You're truly sorry and remorseful for what happened.

The Fuckery that is...

Recommitting.

"You're lucky, you get to be with you all day". - Mitch Carper

I kept telling myself it was just one little slip-up. No big deal, right? It wasn't like we'd gone all the way...

Ah, who was I kidding? I'd cheated on myself. I had to accept it, stop beating myself up over it, and recommit.

Garza and I were texting each other every day, but I didn't let on that I was interested in more than just a friendship. Whenever I was around him, I didn't show any physical affection, or let him do the same to me. About a week after we met, he *did* ask to kiss me while we were in my car, heading to the Vega to watch football with Beth and the regulars; and I did give him a brief little peck. Truth be told, I still wasn't sure how to start that conversation about my just not being ready for another relationship.

I realized Garza was treating me differently than the other guys I'd dated. He was always respectful, never pushy, and he sent me sweet texts nearly every day. Not once did he try to go straight in for sex, or insinuate any interest in making this a friends-with-benefits arrangement. I assure you, Garza wouldn't have a hard time getting laid. He wasn't just smoking hot, but very charming – and in a natural way, not a forced, bullshit type of way. He always sounded genuine when he spoke and listened intently during conversations.

Here we go again, I thought. *Another great guy who checks most of the boxes.* And still, I didn't want anything more with him. At least this time, it wasn't based on Garza not needing anyone to "fix" him; it had to do with my relationship with myself, and the fact that I was exploring my own happiness.

***

Wednesday morning. I woke up at 5:30 AM, going through my morning routine with Bula and coffee before driving out to the beach at sunrise. I was used to being there all by myself, and never expected I'd run into anyone I knew.

As I stood with my feet just barely at the tide, all of a sudden, I heard, "Hey, Ty!"

I turned around to see a guy sitting on the beach by himself. I squinted a bit to get a clearer image of him, soon realizing it was Shaun, one of the regulars from Vega. Shaun was a big guy – he reminded me of a giant-ass teddy bear, with about 260 pounds to his six-foot-four frame – but he was built with a lot of muscle and tone. His arms were probably the size of my thighs, and I have freaking dancer thighs! He was pretty handsome, too, with blonde hair showing a sprinkling of gray and a large, bold face.

"Morning, Shaun!" I said as I approached him. "Do you mind if I join you?"

"Not at all, have a seat!"

I took off my flip flops, strategically placing them about eight inches apart on the sand, one for each of my ass cheeks. I sat down.

"What are you doing out here so early?"

"I've been coming out here every morning for the last week or so," he said. "It's been really nice, waking up early. I haven't been out in a while."

"Yeah, I guess I haven't seen you at Vega, lately. Then again, I only go once a week or so. We're likely to miss each other."

This was the first non-bar-banter conversation I'd had since I moved to Florida. Shaun started to fill me in on some mundane things I hadn't known about him – his family, his sister, how he'd never had a girlfriend.

"You're better off that way, trust me," I said. "Relationships suck!"

"Yeah, but my mom always busts my ass about it."

"It's your decision, either way. I'm sure you could have one if you wanted." My tone became more serious. "Take it from me, what you see in the movies and on TV is bullshit. It's not real."

For another 20 minutes or so, we shared more semi-personal details about who each other were beyond the bar scene. As the sun rose up above the clouds in the distance, I sighed.

"Well, I've gotta go get ready for work. But, Shaun, this was really great. Thank you!"

We walked towards the main road, up the sandy path, and to my car, which was parked right next to his truck. In a snap decision, I asked Shaun if he was any good at trivia.

His face lit up. "Hell yes! I love trivia."

"Perfect! Do you want to join my friend and I for quiz night at the 26 Degrees Brewery? It starts at 7:00 PM."

"Yeah, absolutely!"

We exchanged numbers, then took off in different directions. Shaun would never be someone I was interested in romantically; but he'd be a good friend, for sure.

The Fuckery that is...

Honesty.

"Think of all the time in the world that has been wasted by lies. Fuck, that's a lot of time." – Ty Paige

That friend I mentioned I was going to trivia night with? If you guessed Garza, you'd be absolutely right.

I figured, if we could just step outside for a few minutes, I'd be able to talk to him and let him down easy. Keeping it casual seemed like the best idea: acknowledging his interest but letting him know I just wasn't ready to date anyone. It felt like a huge fucking copout – you know, that whole "it's not you, it's me" bullshit that people use as an excuse not to date someone – except for me, it was the truth. I liked Garza a hell of a lot; but, as things stood, I couldn't be with anyone other than me.

We all arrived – Garza, Shaun, and I – and grabbed a small table just as the quiz started. We proved to be a powerful little trivia team, nailing all the different subjects, even going up against teams of eight or so players.

When the host announced intermission, I asked Garza if he'd come out with me for a few minutes.

"So… I just want to keep this short, but real," I began, staring into his gorgeous, sparkling eyes.

"Okay."

I took a deep breath. "I haven't dated anyone since I went through a really abusive relationship, with a guy I filed criminal charges against. For aggravated assault and domestic violence."

"Oh. Oh my gosh, okay."

"Yeah… And I've been hyper-focused on just being single since then, which was back in the spring. I like you. I promise I do. But I'm not healed yet, and I don't want to lead you on. I just… I can't date right now."

Garza looked a little disappointed.

"I know this sounds like bullshit," I went on. Everything he'd done over the past few weeks had been so gentle, so appropriate, I didn't want him to think he had done anything wrong. "I get it. But it is *not* you, it is 100% me. Hell, you have everything I'd want in a guy, but the timing just isn't right. I need to stay focused on myself until I feel like I'm able to be touched again. What I went through was *that bad.*"

With his sucker-me-in accent, he said, "I'm so sorry you went through that. I understand. I really like you too. I haven't dated in a while, myself – I've been working on myself, too. So, I get it."

I felt a weight lift off my shoulders. Thank fuck, I wasn't going to lose him completely. We could still be friends. Maybe if the timing was right, later, something more could happen. For now, we'd still text each other, and meet up for drinks occasionally, and stick to our just-platonic pact.

That was, until one night at Vega, a few weeks later…

***

Friday. Garza had gotten off work early that day, and he'd gone to Vega to drink with his colleagues during the afternoon. I'd agreed to meet him there in the evening, but I wouldn't be there until after 7:00 PM, since I'd have to run home to take Bula for a walk after work.

By the time I arrived, I could tell Garza was *wasted*. As soon as I entered, he pulled me in and put his arm around me, introducing me to his colleague, whose greeted me with a cheery, "I've heard so much about you!"

Uh oh.

Regardless of how crazy fucking handsome he looked in his dark blue suite, I spent the rest of the night warding him off, reminding him, more than once, "Hey, you know, we aren't dating, and you are being really handsy with me." He wasn't being forceful at all, but if you were a nearby patron, you'd have thought we were a couple from the way he was touching me.

The final straw came when, while I was ordering a glass of water, he confessed his feelings for me.

"I haven't felt like this for anyone in a long time," he slurred.

Oh, fuck, Garza. Do we need to have the conversation again? Shit, maybe we do.

***

I decided to distance myself a little, after that. I stopped hanging out with him as often and would even ignore his texts for hours, hoping he'd realize on his own that he'd gone against what we'd agreed to on trivia night. I did discuss what had gone down at Vega with him, just to reiterate that my feelings for myself were greater than my feelings to date anyone.

Over the next couple months, we still met up now and then; but with the reaffirmed, mutual understanding that, for the foreseeable future, we wouldn't be anything more than friends.

The Fuckery that is...

The Bucket List.

"Relying on people will let you down but relying on your passion and talent won't. Go do what you love, and fuck people."
– Ty Paige

November came. I'd booked a solo, overnight trip to Washington, DC for a Genesis concert. It was the only gig left on my (current) bucket list – I'd loved Phil Collins and his music ever since I was a kid, and I wasn't about to pass up a chance to see him and his band live! So, I took the day completely off work: flying up to DC, exploring the city, and heading to the concert in the evening.

Sure, I'd traveled by myself, all over the US, in the past ten or so years; but it'd always been for work. I'd never taken a trip by myself that was purely for leisure. Since my plans for Thailand and Bali fell through – and with everything that had happened since – I hadn't had much chance to think about it.

***

My flight into Regan Airport landed before noon, and the Uber ride to my downtown hotel took just over 10 minutes. I was able to check in to my room early, which was awesome. I'd already mapped out all the landmarks I wanted to visit, and figured I'd definitely need a few hours to reach them on foot.

I slung my backpack onto the couch, setting down all my burdens. I let out a shriek of excitement, started dancing around, laughing. Holy fuck – I was all by myself, in a new city, for an entire day. I could do anything, whatever the hell I wanted! I let loose, totally swept up in the freedom I'd worked so hard to achieve, shimmying over to the bed, leaping up, and jumping up and down like a little kid, before ass-planting the mattress and laying out like a starfish. I took a deep breath.

You're here. You got this, Ty, I thought. *Go enjoy your day.*

And I sure as hell did, spending hours upon hours walking around our nation's capital. I snapped some souvenir photos as I went past the White House, then took my sweet time wandering the various exhibits at the Smithsonian Museum. From there, I made my way to the Washington Monument and Veteran's Park, which both captured me in ways I can't even describe. I stopped at Veteran's Park for a while, touching my fingers to the fountain in honor of my late grandfather, who served in World War II.

The winding path leading to the Lincoln Memorial was lined with huge, fully blossomed trees. A mild breeze drifted about me, sending a few showers of petals spiraling down towards the ground.

"Thank you," I wanted to whisper to each of them; to every blade of grass, every crack in the sidewalk. I felt almost as if the city were welcoming me, embracing me, letting me know it appreciated the courage it took to come here all by myself. I drew strength from the stunning grounds and the memory of the ancestors who'd walked here before me.

As I climbed the stairs to the memorial, I couldn't help recalling what "Honest Abe" stood for. The lies I'd been told by John, and the bullshit lies Blake was still spreading… Both ghosts of my past rose up, beginning to overwhelm me as I stared up at the statue. I had a BAC moment.

Belief: People lie when the truth is a bad reflection of who they really are.

Action: People can change, and when they do, it proves that they really love you.

Challenge: Leave after the first fucking lie. *Leave!*

I wished I had more time to explore every last corner of DC, but it was getting late. I had to go get ready for Genesis!

***

The concert was nothing short of amazing. Phil Collins didn't disappoint – if anything, his performance was all the more impressive, considering he could no longer stand and wasn't as mobile as he used to be.

I sang all the words I'd burned into my brain across the decades; I danced along with everyone in the concert hall; I took a couple of live videos to share with my friends online (and, of course, to evidence that I'd been there!). Holy shit – I did this all for *me*. I bought a single ticket to the gig, flew up here, and now here I am, having the time of my life! I was on top of the world, feeling as if there wasn't anything I couldn't do.

I stumbled out into the fresh air, went to the closest restaurant to order a cheeseburger and onion rings to go, had a beer, and headed back to my room to eat and fall asleep after the best. Day. Ever.

That cheeseburger was fucking awesome, too, in case you were wondering.

**

My DC adventure was tons of fun, but it wasn't enough. I'd seriously caught the solo travel bug, and I needed to take another trip – something bigger, something way outside my comfort zone!

When I got back home, I did some research through the Facebook group I'd relied upon a couple years prior, Girls Love Travel. There were multiple posts, by fellow solo female travelers, about Guatemala. Specifically, Antigua and the multiple villages surrounding the beautiful Lake Atitlan. They all said they felt safe and comfortable, there, and *Oh my God,* their photos were just unbelievable.

I did have my reservations – who wouldn't, if they'd never traveled alone outside their home country? – but I decided, fuck it, I was going to do it! I'd waited years for something like this.

I had no commitments, no responsibilities aside from my job (and Bula girl!). I had a "skeleton week" coming up at the agency, from Christmas through New Year's, where I'd pretty much be free. So, after a lot of research and asking for advice in the group, I hit that shiny "book" button. Holy shit – I was going to Guatemala!

The Fuckery that is...

Christmas.

"Some people will stop loving you when you start to love yourself. Perhaps the only thing they loved was seeing you struggle." – Ty Paige

I had plenty of time to plan out my loose agenda and mentally prepare for my first major, solo vacation. Of course, when I shared the news with my friends, they all told me I was crazy. Mostly, they were concerned I'd be kidnapped or trafficked, but I just laughed as I thought, *Who the hell wants to kidnap a divorcee who talks too much?*

I kept pushing their – and my own – fears aside, and the week of Christmas soon arrived. I was all packed and ready to go. My stomach was in knots, and I swear that morning-flight mimosa was the only thing that calmed me enough to push myself onto the plane.

I posted a photo of me and my drink, smiling through my nerves, to social media. The caption said it all:

Here I Gooooooo!

As the comments flooded in, some in encouragement and others in worry, I flew off to Guatemala City.

***

When I boarded the flight, I quickly realized I was one of the only tourists on board. I'd say over 95% of the travelers aboard my flight were Guatemalan, and here I was, sitting in Row One, with my blonde hair and bright green eyes making me stick out like a sore thumb. An uneasy feeling settled deep in my gut as I pulled out my phone, threw my headphones in, and put on some familiar episodes of *Friends*.

However, my mood shifted as we began to descend. This was my trip, I reminded myself. I was ready to rock it, and holy fuck, was I going to! We touched down, and I made my way through the airport, basking in the colorful hustle and bustle around me. Groups of locals were crowding in the arrivals hall, spilling onto the street outside, with balloons and flowers and big smiles. I'd never seen anything like it back home, and a huge grin broke out over my own face as I walked through the sea of people, looking for my name on one of the cab drivers' signs. I even had my camera out, ready to snap a pic of the historic occasion – hey, I'd never had anyone waiting for me like that, before!

Thirty minutes later, I was still searching for my taxi. I checked in with the company through their WhatsApp. No response. I started to get a little panicky; but I had seen some other cabs parked up that looked legitimate. So, if all else failed, I could always ask a gate agent to verify one for me and get on my way to Antigua, the first stop of my trip.

If we live in a world where we're meant to follow the signs, this wasn't a good one (pun entirely intended). *Well, Ty,* I thought, *not all those signs are so blatant that they have your name directly on them.*

Wait a second…

I took one last stroll through the arrivals area, and, yep, there he was! A man holding a sign that read *MAESTROS DE TYLAR.* Ha. Yeah, I guess that's me! Sometimes, our signs are still there, but they're a little out of order. At least my first name was right. That gave me comfort.

The guy quickly grabbed my bright green carry-on suitcase and ushered me to the car. He'd just started to drive away, making small talk with me, when he got a call that, in fact, he wasn't meant to be my driver. We turned around, I got out – and he left with my suitcase still in the trunk. Well, shit. I hadn't even been there an hour, and I was already a theft victim!

Luckily, I turned out to be very wrong. He was just taking my luggage to the other vehicle, with the assigned driver, for me. Facepalm.

I got in the right cab, and Vinny, who was from Guatemala but had lived in the States previously, Vermont to be exact, finally got us the hell away from the airport. The traffic wasn't as bad as usual, from what he told me, thank God.

Then again, it was Christmas Day.

***

The drive to Antigua took about 45 minutes, and the entire ride was filled with great conversation and hilarious stories. At one point, Bon Jovi's *Living on a Prayer* came on the radio, and I burst out singing.

"Oh, do you like karaoke?" Vinny asked.

"I usually need a couple drinks in me before I do it, but yeah!"

"You're not very good!"

My attempt at belting out those iconic lyrics dissolved into laughter. Usually, when I go to karaoke nights, I just pick a song where I can show off my dance skills, to deflect from my obvious lack of musical talent. It was kind of refreshing to hear someone be honest with me about it!

We arrived at my hotel in Antigua, and I was struck by a feeling of complete awe. Lush gardens; antique décor and furniture; ornate stairs; paintings and embellishments with colors galore – all designed around a cluster of beautiful trees that must have been hundreds of years old. Even the key to my room was an actual vintage: metal, handmade, almost too large to fit in my hand. It took some fiddling to get the old key to fit in the lock, but I finally succeeded.

It was heaven. I lunged onto the bed and started giggling. Perhaps I was decompressing after feeling so nervous earlier. Perhaps I still couldn't quite believe that I'd finally fucking done it. Or it could have been that I was simply happy.

After I freshened up a little, I stepped out to start wandering the sublime streets of Antigua, with no clue where I was going or what I'd be getting myself into.

The buildings boasted a veritable rainbow of colors, and the narrow, one-way streets were filled with congregations of vibrantly dressed locals. My hotel was close to the famous Santa Catalina Arch, so, naturally, I steered myself straight in that direction.

As I approached the landmark, which was painted a gorgeous golden-yellow and topped by its own personal, domed clocktower, I got a very familiar feeling that was difficult to identify. I was sure that, at some point, I'd recognize it; but this wasn't the moment.

I continued strolling, narrowly dodging the people, cars, and bikes whizzing by so fast they'd paste you to the ground if you weren't paying attention. The vehicles at the sides of the roads were parallel parked so tightly, it was tough to find a clear spot to cross.

I was about to shimmy between two parked cars when I felt a tingle, like a light splashing, on my foot. Oh my God, it was pee! A man was peeing on the street, right where I was walking! I jumped back and kept going, pretending I hadn't noticed anything. I figured I might as well just carry on – my feet were bound to need a solid, independent shower of their own, anyway, when I got back to the hotel.

I headed back towards the arch and continued down that way, eventually reaching the Iglesias Church, which was nestled next to a gorgeous central area with a fountain and vendors galore. I sat on a bench to people-watch for a little while, before entering the church itself and marveling at the flagstone floor and soaring white pillars supporting the high roof. When I emerged, I threw a quetzal (the main coin of currency) into the fountain and made a wish. I'd end up doing this several more times throughout my trip, in random fountains, with my wish always being the same. I'm sure you're dying to know what it was; but you know if I told you, it wouldn't come true, right?

As I retraced my steps, I spotted a small entryway – a sort of cement arch that looked somewhat out of place. Beyond it lay some ruins; and inside, there was an exhibit on display. A gentleman was standing at the entry, taking donations. I slid a few quetzals into the donation bucket and walked into what would end up being a life-changing thirty minutes.

Growing up, we didn't celebrate Christmas like most families. I never got to feel the rush of waking up to a bright, shiny tree with presents spilling out from underneath it. Our holidays always felt more like obligations, or a chore. Christmas, as I'd come to know it, was really about the birth of Jesus. This exhibit, which displayed a different image of the pain Jesus Christ suffered every five feet, brought me to tears.

This was a Christmas I needed, one that really touched my heart. No gifts, no presents, no money, no songs, no cheer, no joy, no tree, no ornaments. Just a sheer movement in myself, a moment where I felt so thankful and loved. As much as I swear, or sin, or make bad decisions, in my heart, I'm a Christian and believer. As my old pastor used to remind me: "Keep one foot in the church and one foot in the real world." But right there, right then, I felt the same love that Jesus felt when he died for us.

I needed a drink.

The Fuckery that is...

Not Being Kidnapped.

"Don't listen to what they say. Go see." – Chinese Proverb

I popped into a very small pub across the street from the exhibit. The bartender offered me a local brew called Antigua Noble, and since I only drink painfully light beers that cater to my Type-A personality, I said, "Sure!" It was a very crisp, lighthearted lager, kind of similar to Yuengling, an American beer I've been known to enjoy.

I sat at the bar, which was inside, next to a large, open door, sipping on beer, watching people swirling about outside. There were about ten tables, and about three or four of them were occupied with groups of friends laughing and eating and drinking merrily. Yes, I used the word "merrily" – it was fucking Christmas Day!

Knowing all too well the feeling of being treated like shit when you're alone in the pub, I was pleasantly surprised by how friendly and responsive the bartender was; and everyone who passed by me would flash a smile as if to say, "good for you, girl!". It made my first day on this big solo trip feel exactly as I'd hoped – like it was the best decision of my life. But the day was still young, and I had much more on my agenda!

***

I went back to my castle of a hotel room to change for the evening. I'd booked a romantic dinner for one at the rooftop terrace restaurant – taking myself out, as per my re-commitment!

I slipped on my pink-and-green floral, floor-length maxi dress and leisurely climbed the stairs to the terrace. I sat alone at a table for two, admiring the jaw-dropping, panoramic views of the city and the volcanoes rising up in the distance. Just as my authentic, Guatemalan-style enchilada dinner was set in front of me, Mount Fuego began to erupt.

Holy shit! I couldn't tear my eyes away from the streaks of red and orange jetting up into the night sky, the plumes of smoke forming an almost otherworldly canvas behind them; but I had to capture this to share with my friends back home. I whipped out my camera, grabbing a bunch of photos and videos while I had the chance.

As I was clicking away, a woman and her father started taking their own shots, standing against the stunning backdrop. In true outgoing-photographer fashion, I offered to take a picture of the two of them together, and it turned from a mini photoshoot to shooting shit with new friends.
John and Jenise were from New York City, on their first big father-daughter trip together. They told me all about their plans – where they'd been and where they were going – and I took a couple mental notes for my own itinerary. It was great to have some

company and hear about life in NYC, especially since I'd always wanted to live there.

***

The temperatures in Antigua tend to drop dramatically as soon as the sun goes away; so, it didn't take long for me to get fucking cold. I went to my room to change into a sweater, asking the NYC folks to meet me at the little brewery across the street for a beer in 30 minutes. This place was barely visible from the street, giving it the air of a cozy spot only the locals knew. And, when we walked in, we met a petite young girl who was working away while cradling an adorable bulldog puppy in one arm. I swear, I like dogs more than people most days; so, of course, I instantly became *that* person who wants to hold and cuddle and love on the puppy before I even knew their human's name.

Cue baby talk to the little one, named Heya, and plenty of photo opportunities. We each ordered a drink, kicked back, and chatted with a couple of locals who were also enjoying some holiday brews.

The sun had set hours ago, and the streets were dim, barely lit by the one-a-block lights. Still, we strutted around the city without a care in the world, popping into a couple of bars to check out the live music and vibes. Eventually, we made our way to La Taverna Bar, the owner of which I'd been virtually introduced to by the Girls Love Travel group.

Aury was a beautiful woman with dark hair, golden skin, and a naturally attractive personality to match. Between countless people coming up to hug her and say hello – it seemed she knew everyone in town! We discussed her business ventures in Antigua, something that naturally interested me as a fellow entrepreneur. Along with my New York buddies, I stayed for a couple drinks and fun games with some of the other patrons.

Since I knew I'd be walking back to my hotel alone, I kept my alcohol intake to a minimum. Even when the rest of our little group started playing "Thunderstruck" – where they play the AC/DC song, and whenever Brian Johnson says "thunder!", you've got to drink until he says it again and someone else takes over chugging duty – I opted to video the shenanigans. No way was I going to spend my first night on this solo trip drunk as fuck! Besides, I had plans to wake up early and walk to the Ruinas de La Recolleción for a sunrise photoshoot.

The night was, quite frankly, fucking fantastic. John, Jenise and I met new people from all over the world, including a chatty guy named Ricardo who gave me a much-needed hug – not a romantic or intimate embrace, just a big, friendly bear squeeze that he'd never fully understand the significance of.

Aury had also introduced us to Joseph. While originally from Syria, he'd lived in Guatemala for many years, building a career as a professional motorcycle rider. He'd won countless championships and traveled all over the world. Standing at no more than five-foot-nine and even skinnier than my 140-pound frame, Joseph still managed to have an attractiveness about him that drew me in, I admit, just a little bit.

I still had no interest in meeting anyone to start a love affair, so we just hung out, small talking our way through the evening much like I was doing with everyone else. At one point, though, I mentioned my friends' concerns about me traveling alone.
"Yeah, this solo trip has a lot of my friends back home really

worried."

"Oh, why is that?"

"They all think I'm going to get kidnapped." I couldn't help but laugh. "I assured them no one wants an old divorcee who talks too much."

"I'm also divorced, once," Joseph commented. "But they say you talk too much?"

"I *know* I do!"

"Well, I would kidnap you!"

A bit of a weird remark, but it was his subtle way of flirting with me, and I found it kind of cute. About five minutes later, though, he did admit: "Okay, you're right. You talk too much!"

We chatted a little more about nothing in particular, exchanged Instagram follows, and I thought that was the end of it.

If you've been keeping up with my track record, you already know I was wrong.

I got back to my room around 10:30 PM. Exhausted from the long day of travel, sightseeing, picture-taking, new friendships, and drinks, I stripped down and didn't even put my pajamas on. I sprawled out like a starfish on the queen-size bed, completely naked, and slept like a baby.

The Fuckery that is...

Moza.

"Don't dismiss something you get that you didn't ask for. It could turn out to have more meaning than you ever imagined and be exactly what you need." – Ty Paige

I woke up to the fresh smells of scrambled eggs and tortillas, the traditional Guatemalan breakfast, wafting through my open windows. I damn near leaped out of bed. What was my second day here going to bring? I was sure it could only get better – I mean, fuck, the first one had nearly busted my fun meter! My plan was to put on a cute, yet conservative, outfit and walk all the way to the edge of town, where a series of earthquakes had conveniently turned the Ruinas de La Recollección into the perfect place to take phenomenal self-portraits.

I swear, everything I buy these days is from Amazon Prime – it's pretty much become my permanent personal shopping assistant, so I rarely ever get anything that doesn't fit or isn't my style.
I left my room wearing a gorgeous off-the-shoulder ruffled white blouse, one that could easily be midriff with a little upward tug, with high-waisted, tight-fitting jeans that made my "Sad Ass Syndrome" a little less obvious. My ass is the living embodiment

of that emoji with the slanted smile. It's not happy or sad, it's just kind of "meh", like half of the time it doesn't fucking know or care what's going on.

Anyway, I grabbed a coffee-to-go from the neighboring shop, and leisurely made my way to the church, passing some already-familiar spots. Yep, through the arch once again, which was still resonating that weirdly familiar, undefinable feeling. With the cobblestone road beneath my pink Amazon Essentials flip flops, I walked to the edge of civilization – where, had it not been daylight, I might have felt more than a tad uncomfortable.

There it was. The massive stone structure that had once been a church, made even more beautiful by its near-total destruction.

I paid the 20 quetzals to enter and soon realized I was the only person there. I walked the grounds, staring up at these ruins that resembled some kind of ancient climbing frame. I couldn't resist. I strategically set up my portable iPhone tripod, grabbed the Bluetooth clicker, and scrambled up.

After a modest fifteen-minute photoshoot of myself, I headed back to town to finally get my hands on some of that delicious breakfast food. I popped into a little café, which was also like a pub; and, since I was, after all, on vacation, I figured I might as well say "fuck it" and order a delicious Guatemalan mimosa. What arrived at my table, however, was decidedly not what I'd asked for.

I looked at the glass of bock beer, then up at the waiter.

"What is this?" I asked him.

"Moza!"

This couldn't have been a clearer encounter of the language barrier if it came with huge, flashing neon lights and a parade's worth of red flags. I glanced back at the beer. Back at the waiter.

"I asked for a mimosa?" I sort of posed as a question with what I'm sure was a strange look on my face.

"Sí, a Moza!" he cheeringly insisted.

In the end, I couldn't really do anything except laugh off the confusion and drink the damn Moza.

Curious as to what the name meant in Spanish, I opened my translation app and tapped in *moza*.

Girl.

Moza. Girl. Singular. *Me.*

No, this couldn't be a mishap. The coincidence was just... too fucking convenient. This was what my life had become. Me, a single girl, in a foreign country, all by herself, enjoying a – *me.*

***

Funky name aside, it really was quite a tasty beer; and it gave me a slight boost of energy for my next excursion – the shuttle ride to Panajachel, a village about two-and-a-half hours away on Lake Atitlán.

I hopped aboard the packed, yet very quiet, bus and chose a seat by the door, right in front of a younger guy with long, curly blonde hair and sparkling blue eyes that appeared to be closer together than most people's. I may be in my forties, but I can still hold the attention of guys in their late twenties or early thirties!

His name was Yul, and he was from Germany. On the bench next to him sat a Polish girl in her mid-thirties, named Erin, with whom I soon struck up a conversation. She had blonde hair, too; and she looked much like a younger version of my ex-husband's ex-girlfriend, so I asked if she was American.

"No, but I'm living in Miami, at the moment."

"Oh, wow!" I exclaimed. "We're neighbors!"

All at once, it seemed, everyone on the bus began chatting. When we stopped at a gas station on the edge of town, Yul, Erin, and I snagged a couple beers for the ride. We jumped back into our seats, toasting the start of our long journey with a "Cheers!".

The road to Panajachel is not only extremely windy and terrifying, but also very depressing. I saw animals tied up on the side of the road, countless families with children waiting for drivers passing by to throw quetzals to them. I'd given the driver all my loose change to donate, and my heart broke every single time, seeing the kids scurry to pick up the coins.

We'd all agreed we needed a bathroom break about 45 minutes prior to arriving, so we stopped at a tiny little street lined with vendors and shops. They charged us two quetzals each to use the bathroom, which was actually more like a bucket behind a wooden door. I think I was the one who had to pee the worst, so I gave the man twenty quetzals and paid for every one of us to have the privilege of experiencing this rather unique toilet.

The man escorted us around to the back of the shop, and my eyes widened. The scenery was fucking unreal! We were high atop a mountain, overlooking miles of other mountains, trees, small bodies of water, and colors galore. One by one, we alternated phones to take pictures of each other, standing on what felt like the top of the fucking world.

I went into the makeshift stall first, keeping my head above the door, cracking jokes about it being the best bathroom view I've ever had. One by one, we finished our "bucket business", with the man emptying them out in between breaks.

It wasn't much longer until the shuttle was dropping me off in the bustling village I'd call home for the next few days.

***

Lake Atitlán is often referred to as "the most beautiful lake in the world", and I'd already spent plenty of time researching exactly what I wanted to see and do while there. Panajachel – which locals shortened to simply "Pana" – had one main, mile-long, narrow road lined with street vendors and shops. I'd decided to stay at a small, quaint hotel, ensuring I'd be central enough to go sightseeing, by boat, in the surrounding area, and not feel too terribly secluded.

The path there was slightly paved, flanked by smiling locals going about their daily business. As I went to check in, I was greeted by a squawk from the reception desk.

"Hola!"

Turned out the hotel had their own talking parrot, named Polly. I chuckled, saying "Hola!" right back.

Once I'd gotten settled in and changed, I stopped by the market on the main street for a cold beer before heading to Lake Atitlán, which was just a short walk away. Perhaps surprisingly, I wasn't hounded by any of the vendors as I walked down the street, looking more out of place than a streaker running down the field during a Monday Night Football game.

The sight of the shimmering, azure water, stirring softly in the giant crater that held it, framed by the rugged sweeps of the volcanoes around it, took my breath away. I'd worn a rhinestone camisole that I'd embellished by hand, just to get a photo wearing it by the lake. I snapped a somewhat successful selfie and filmed a quick video of the scene; then, I spent the best part of an hour just relaxing, taking in the views and people-watching.

***

The sun was about to set, and I was getting kind of hungry. On my way back towards Pana, I found a restaurant with views of the lake, serving the local food and beer I was eager to try out. I grabbed a table, sat my ass down, and waited.

Remember when I said that dining alone pretty much guarantees you crappy service? Yeah, that held very true for this particular place. It took over 45 minutes to get my food order taken, then another hour for my meal to arrive. Meanwhile, the two other tables, filled by parties of four and ten, respectively, were being tended to almost constantly, with laughs and smiles to boot.

Nearly two hours had gone by, and all I'd been served was one beer when I first arrived, and my (rather delicious) chicken, mushroom, and spinach alfredo. I waited and waited for the server to bring my check; but I eventually gave up. I left the proper amount of quetzals on the table, walked back to my room, threw a Netflix show on my phone, and went to bed at just 7:30 PM.

The Fuckery that is...

A Hostel Party.

"There is no definition of beauty, but when you can see someone's spirit coming through, something unexplainable, that's beautiful to me." – Liv Tyler

I had just enough time, the next morning, to make it down to the lake and grab a spot near the docks to watch the sunrise. It was crazy how empty the streets were so early in the morning, when they were packed so tightly the day before you had zero personal space.

The hour I spent watching the sun come up, painting vivid streaks of pink, orange, and gold between the volcanoes, was one of much-needed reflection. It was wonderfully quiet, with the only sounds coming from a Christmas tree that had musical lights on it. Sounds kind of cool, right?

What if I told you that each string of lights had its own song, and that there must've been at least five of them, all playing at once?

Yikes. That tree needed a fresh prescription of Ritalin, or perhaps a roofie.

I grabbed my satchel to head back down to the lake, where there were several lanchas – from which the boat taxis embarked – and purchased a round trip to San Pedro. The vessel was small, and it was packed with local families, who laughed and pointed at the water splashing up around us as we carved a swift path across the lake. I guess they rode these things on a regular basis; but I, for one, wasn't entirely sure we weren't going to sink.

After a stop in San Marcos, where man buns are aplenty, and San Juan, we sailed over to my main destination.

The trek up to the principal village was steep, although the path was paved and dotted with tons of tourist spots. As intriguing as they were, I'd come prepared with my own agenda. Good thing I was willing to go with the flow, because my itinerary had wrenches thrown into it all day long.

I went straight to the Tzunun'Ya museum, which was closed due to COVID, then hiked up to the top of the mountain to Los Termales (thermal spas). The area you pass through to reach Los Termales can feel a bit sketchy if you're a woman walking all by yourself; so, I eventually decided to turn around and go back down to the touristy area. A bit disappointing, but what the hell. Might as well enjoy the views and have lunch!

While soaking up the sun at a little restaurant, Franco, the owner, offered me a free beer. Just as I was accepting it, two guys walked in and sat near me.

"Hey, would you mind taking a photo of me?" I asked them.

"Sure, no problem!" said one of them, in a Miami accent.

"Oh, you speak English! Thank you!"
I handed over my phone in camera mode, stepped back to the deck railing, turned my body to the side, and sucked my stomach in (we all do it, ladies!) as he snapped away. I couldn't help noticing that they were giving me odd looks, like they thought it was strange for me to be alone in San Pedro.

The other guy handed my phone back to me.

"Are you from America?" I asked.

"Yeah, are you?" Sounded like he was from the Midwest. As it turned out, he was from Chicago.

"Yep! I'm just here on a little solo vacation."

"Wow, that's really cool! We just got here yesterday, took the shuttle from Guatemala City to Pana then a private ferry here to San Pedro."

He pulled out his phone, showing me some of the photos they'd taken while riding across the lake.

"Oh my gosh, those are great!" I exclaimed. "I took a shared boat this morning from Pana. My photos are nowhere near this awesome."

"It was pretty cool," Miami chipped in. "The driver just let us tell him where we wanted to go, and we got to perch up on the front of the boat, so we had the *best* views!"

Damn! I'd definitely fucked up a little, there. "Maybe I should take a private ride back, and just consider my round trip ticket a loss."

"You definitely should!" Chicago agreed.

"We're actually heading to Pana later today," his buddy said. "How is it? We didn't stop in, really – just went straight to the lancha to get here."

"It's really busy, but I didn't find much to do there last night. Maybe because I was by myself, I don't know…"

**

We sat together for over an hour, bantering, story-sharing, and laughing. Both guys had studied at the University of Michigan, so we had a lot to talk about, given that I'd lived in Detroit for nearly twenty years. Of course, being a Michigan State Spartans fan myself, I set out on a mission to get at least one "Go White!" out of them after I'd yell "Go Green!"

Yeah, that was a bust.

I told them about my failed excursion to Los Termales, and they seemed super-excited to check it out. So, the three of us splurged on a tuktuk (an open-air taxi about half the size of a Smartcar) and rode up to the El Barrio Restaurant, at the bottom of the trail to the pools. Fortunately, Chicago was fluent in Spanish, and he easily scored us a tub chatting with the lady who ran the thermals, who spoke zero English.

I changed into my swimsuit, and we all climbed into the blissfully warm water. This wasn't just any hot tub – it was a thermal stone one, manually-filled, and situated at the top point of San Pedro, overlooking the lake. The lush gardens all around created a stunning border for the distant volcanoes.

I settled back with a contented sigh. After reading all the glowing Google reviews, this had been one of my top priorities for my trip; and had I not met Chicago and Miami, I'd most likely have never made it there. Maybe there really are no chance meetings!

***

After a nice soak in the thermal, we headed back down to the lancha to start negotiating a good price for a private boat to Pana. We managed to secure one for about $10 USD per person; and I changed into a two-piece dress I'd packed, an outfit I was adamant I wanted photos in while on the lake. We staged pictures and videos, danced, and sang our hearts out for the entire thirty-minute cruise.

When we made it back to dry land, the guys took a taxi to their hotel, and I went in search of some much-needed food. There was a little pizzeria right by the path to my hotel, so I dropped in, ordering one of my favorite Italian dishes – a calzone.

I hate to admit it, but it was a pretty sad calzone, small and not very filling. However, I did catch a bit of a second wind from it; and, after a fantastic power nap where it settled into my tummy, I was ready to take Erin up on her invitation to a rooftop party at Dream Boat, a nearby hostel.

Now, I wasn't sure what to expect at this get-together, being forty-two years old and having never stayed in a hostel before. At my age, I felt a little awkward going there in the first place! But, as Erin and I walked up to the door, we were greeted by a ruggedly handsome man, who pointed us to the stairs. Erin and I exchanged glances – you know, the kind girls share when we subtly agree "yep, this guy is hot!" – and I thought, perhaps, this night would be pretty fun, after all.

For some Godforsaken reason, the stairs to these rooftop terraces in Guatemala are so terrifyingly narrow and spirally. As we crept up them, I couldn't help but wonder if they were designed like this on purpose, to make you second-guess drinking too much. I'll tell you right now, there's no way in hell I'd make it down those stairs if I were overserved.

Anyway, we managed to get ourselves settled at the bar and order some drinks. I *had* been told to bring my swimsuit, because there was a pool on the rooftop, but the chilly night air – and the fact I was surrounded by girls in their mid-to-late twenties! – kept me from *that* bad decision.

Erin and I were joined by her new friends she'd met hiking earlier that day: Michal, Michael, and Kirin. Before I knew it, there were at least seven other people sitting with us, and we were all chatting about where we were from, our jobs, families, and travels. I will say, while everyone else was decidedly younger than me, not one person flinched at my forty-two-year-old ass being there. One girl was even taken aback when I told her my age! Then again, most people assume I'm in my mid-thirties, so I guess it shouldn't have come as a huge surprise.

As much fun as I was having, I had to work remote the next day and really didn't need to be out late getting plastered with a fresh-out-of-college crowd. I left fairly early, around 10:00 PM, when the crappy-calzone boost had long since worn off. I was craving some seriously greasy food, so I grabbed a sandwich from one of the street vendors on my way home. The owner made me a delicious dish straight from the grill, boxing it up for me to carry it down the rigid brick path. Just the aroma of this calorie-ridden naughty decision was enough to make me feel like I gained five pounds!

I devoured the entire thing in my room, put on my sleepy-time thunder and lightning sounds, and went to bed full and happy.

Damn. What a night. I'd have to look into booking a hostel on my next trip!

The Fuckery that is...

Art.

"Art is so much like my life. The way I see it is never the same as someone else does." – Ty Paige

I woke up early and stepped out to the terrace, where I'd set up my workstation for the day. I was scheduled for the same shift as the other director on my team – a woman whose personality was different from my own. Polly, the talking parrot, had flown up to keep me company – perched on the tree branch behind me, shouting out "Hello!" and "Hola!" every now and then. I sent my colleague a message about her and her antics.

That's not a bad place to work.

She replied.

I was slightly put off that she didn't ask a single question about how my trip was going, or if I was having fun. She'd taken a tropical vacation a few months prior, and when she'd come online to check in on agency business, I asked to see photos and even jokingly said, "Have a drink for us stuck here back in the office!"

Seemed like the polite thing to do, since I spent nearly 40 hours a week working alongside her. Oh, well. Guess I couldn't expect everyone to have the same heart as I did.

***

I'd originally planned to stay in Pana another night; but I'd seen and done everything I wanted to already and was ready to go back to Antigua. Plus, there was a bit of a drought in social activities in the village – not much chance for me to get out after dark!

The shuttle back to Antigua was a fucking nightmare. I jumped aboard thinking it'd be much like the shuttle ride I'd taken into Pana. I'd even packed a beer for the road! But this bus took a different route back, filled with so many tight turns at uncomfortable speeds that I nearly threw up at least ten times.

After the first two hours, and with my anxiety still spiking through the roof, I cracked open that damn beer to try and calm my nerves. As I sipped – or did my best to, what with the shuttle lurching around, threatening to spill the drink all over me – I traded some lighthearted banter with a freckled, red-haired young guy sitting behind me. He lived in Boston and was also on a solo trip. We swapped a few travel stories, too, which helped me focus on something other than the impending possibility of a crash.

I'm a bit of a Type A if you hadn't noticed. I kept my map open the entire trip, so I could see where we were and what the roads ahead looked like. Finally, we started to inch closer to Antigua; and, after what felt like an eternity, the shuttle pulled up outside my hotel. I'd never been so happy to get out of a vehicle in my life!

This particular place was called Hotel y Arte. I'd been stoked about it since the moment I booked my vacation. The owner had sent me videos and photos beforehand, but they couldn't have hoped to do the real thing justice. As soon as I passed the reception desk, it was like my feet had a mind of their own – I couldn't stop walking, seized by the need to take in every inch of the bright, colorful murals that covered each wall. My artist's eye appreciated every last stroke of detail lining the hallway leading up to the garden terrace, where an old, 1950s-style bicycle was kicked up on the lawn. The lights strung up around the garden illuminated the space with a subtle sparkle, as if they didn't want to outshine the beauty of the greenery and the paintings.

Like almost everything in Antigua, this stunning scene was inconspicuously tucked behind a rather unimpressive door. But once I entered, I fell in love with every piece of décor – and the people, and my room, hell, even the kitchen! It was an artist's dream come true.

The front of the hotel hosted a small market, where I grabbed some potato chips to munch on later. Luis, one of the guys who worked there, escorted me to my room, sharing some ideas with me about where to go that evening. I'd already messaged Joseph and Aury, from La Taverna, and they were eager to meet up again.

Ultimately, I'd planned out this whole crazy adventure to focus on myself; so, I took Luis's advice and hit up Sky Café, on the roof terrace. Only having to take about thirty steps from my room to the bar's staircase – even if it *was* yet another dangerously narrow spiral one – was so fucking cool!

The small bar area had about eight chairs. I snagged one and ordered a water and a beer, and had a brief conversation with the bartender, who didn't speak much English. He was a young Guatemalan guy with a lanky frame and boyishly charming face. We tried using my translation app for a bit, and he told me I was cute! Not the most conventional method of flirting (and a first for me!), but I thought it was pretty sweet.

He insisted we take a photo together; then I paid my tab and left to find Joseph and Aury.

***

I met Joseph at SKÅL (pronounced *skoal*), a Viking-themed bar-slash-Danish-restaurant which was one of the many little venues in the nearby, garden-style complex. We had a drink together, chatting with a few of the other stragglers who'd stumbled across this amazing little spot, as well as some of the local patrons. We all meshed together so well, I didn't want to leave – but Joseph and I had agreed to venture over to La Taverna, where Aury had promised us more singing, dancing, game-playing, and mingling.

I'd intended to get back to my hotel early so I could get a good night's rest. So, around 10:30 PM, I thought I'd best get a snack and head out. I ordered a pizza from a little restaurant; and, while waiting for it to cook, had a great chat with the owner. He was from New England, a fellow football fan, had moved to Antigua some time ago.

I was so wrapped up in conversation I almost didn't notice when Joseph strolled in.

"Hi, Greg!" he said cheerily, as if he and the owner had been friends for years.

The two bantered for a little while, then we went out to the street, I with my precious pizza in hand. Joseph had already offered to make sure I got back safe, and now, he asked if I'd like him to drive me there on his motorcycle.

What the fuck are you doing, Ty?! I thought, as I climbed on the back of his bike. *You've never been on one of these things, before! Is this even safe?*

I must have forgotten, for a moment, that Joseph was a professional racer. Of course I'd be fine – he rode these damn things for a living!

We drove the four or five blocks to my hotel, and, ever a perfect gentleman, Joseph walked me to the door and said goodnight.

***

I ate every last fucking crumb of that pizza. I'd pretty much accepted by this point that my usual diet was screwed, and that, since I *was* on vacation, I might as well eat anything and everything I wanted. I even discovered that I actually do like plantains, even though I never had before. Maybe it was the authenticity of how they were prepared in Guatemala, versus how they were cooked back in the States.

I turned in for the night with *Law and Order* playing quietly on the wall-mounted TV in the background.

The Fuckery that is...

No Lights.

"Maybe you have to know the darkness before you can appreciate the light." – Madeline L'Engle

I woke up at 7:00 AM to complete silence.

I rolled over to check my phone. No notifications. No Wi-Fi, either. The TV had gone off, too, which I just chalked up to it being on a timer. I decided to try and sleep a little longer, since I didn't need to be up for anything in particular.

30 minutes or so later, I heard people talking outside my room, and figured I might as well get up and going. I threw on my cotton shorts, a T-shirt, and flip-flops and went to check out the situation. Luis, who was at the front desk, told me repeatedly, "No lights!" What that meant for me was: *fuck,* no power.

Even though, no less than nine hours prior, I'd scarfed down an entire 10-inch pizza without a single fuck given, I was hungry. Besides, the breakfast included in my hotel booking looked incredible!

I made my way to the kitchen, where two lovely Guatemalan ladies were making breakfast for a couple who were also guests at the hotel.

"Buenas dias!" I greeted.

"Buenas dias!" one of the ladies replied. "Café? Breakfast?"

"Café, por favor, y breakfast un hora."

My Spanish isn't great, but she figured I was asking for a coffee now and breakfast in about an hour. I planned to take my drink and go sit by the street – I'd come to love the sight of the less-crowded, yet still bustling, morning atmosphere of Antigua. Women carried their textiles, spices, and organically grown fruits in baskets on their heads, dressed in gorgeous, colorful gowns and skirts. They smiled, while passing, with such a genuine look, they might as well have been telling me "You are beautiful, have a beautiful day." Kids darted around, playing with soccer balls or riding bikes. Fellow tourists lined the walking paths, making their way to see the historic sites and have brunch.

For just an hour, I wanted to feel the breath of the town while enjoying a cup of coffee.

***

My delicious, hot breakfast came complete with scrambled eggs, fruit, tortillas and beans, and a delicious strawberry-jam-banana toast that I decided I'd *have* to make for myself back home.

The lights still weren't working when I went back to my room. With no windows (the rooms were all inside-facing), I didn't even have any natural light to help me get ready for the day. And so, taking a cue from the Marines to "Improvise, Adapt, and Overcome", I used the flashlight on my phone to take a cold shower and semi-effortlessly put a dab of makeup on my face.

After I got dressed, I sent a message to Joseph.

Hola! There is no power at my hotel, I don't know for how long. I need to charge my phone! If it dies, you can come meet me at the rooftop any time after 1:00 PM. I will be here.

I'd also messaged Erin a similar thing, as we'd been planning to meet up in Antigua, as well.

A couple minutes later, Joseph replied.

Good morning! I have to run errands for my trip tomorrow and then will come meet you at 1:00. If you need to charge your phone, my bar has power.

As I'd since found out, Joseph wasn't only a motorcycle racer. He owned a motorcycle tour company, a bar, *and* an Airbnb property in town. At least I'd have somewhere to go if the issues at the hotel kept up.

I had some time to spare before we were due to meet, so I set out strolling around the town to see the rest of the sights I hadn't seen my first day and half there, trying not to worry about my quickly dying phone battery.

**

As I walked through Parque de Central, I thought I'd never seen so many couples, sitting on benches and openly embracing, or peddlers ever-so-humbly asking if I was interested in buying jewelry or hand-woven scarfs (the latter of which I'd already purchased in San Pedro). I *did* want to buy myself a pair of earrings; but I tend to wear simple jewelry, and most of the street vendors had very ornate pieces. They were beautiful, but not my taste. And so, I politely said, "No, gracias," as I headed towards the nearest ATM.

After getting some cash, I dived into the central market right beside the Parque de Central. One of the first stalls I saw had a lot of accessories laid out, and I found myself drawn to a pair of heart-shaped jade earrings set in white gold. My favorite color and shaped in the perfect symbol of loving myself. Yes. Those were the ones.

I handed over a few quetzals, pocketed my prize, and turned to leave. Well, I *thought* I was leaving. Because of COVID, arrows had been painted on the floor to direct visitors, turning the maze of shops and stalls into a one-way system. The longer I walked, the more hopeless and trapped I felt, like I was in a labyrinth with a single escape point I had no chance of finding. I picked up my pace, my chest tightening, my breath coming fast, eventually retracing my steps in a resounding "fuck you" to the arrows. A mismatched chorus of shouts from the vendors pummeled my ears. I kept going. I didn't want to disregard the safety rules, but I *had* to get out before I had a full-blown panic attack.

Finally, I saw light at the end of the tunnel, or, well, the walkway, which had become much like a tunnel. I stepped out into the fresh air, pulled my mask off my face, and let out a huge breath of relief.

***

I needed a major reset, so I took my time wandering through the park, past the fountain, and over to Antigua's main church. Its doors were open all the time, and visitors – tourists and locals alike – could walk in and sit down on one of its many decorative, hand-carved pews. I took a seat near the middle, and just breathed, in and out, for at least five minutes. I said prayers for many people in my life that needed them, including myself. I opened my eyes, took in the spirituality of the interior, the history and culture it represented, and got up to walk around.

Lit candles stood everywhere, and colorful curtains hung around crosses and hand-made statues of Jesus, Mary, and Joseph. I felt God with me in that moment, and I'd never felt more at peace. This trip had already opened my eyes to how whole I felt as a person, how I could feel confident and comfortable in my own skin and with my own decisions. Here, in this church, I found myself oddly in love with my own solitude.

***

It was just past lunchtime, and I headed back to my hotel. The power was still out, and I was down to about 30 percent battery life. I sent Joseph another message:

Hey! I'm back to my hotel, still no power. I have to get my Covid test at 2:00 but will be on the rooftop if you want to join me.

Yes I will be there in 10 minutes.

He replied. Nothing in Antigua was further than 10 minutes by vehicle.

True to his word, Joseph came to the Sky Café, and we shared an afternoon beer before I went for my test. I had to show proof of a negative COVID test to travel back to the States the following day. I was a little nervous I'd get a false positive and end up stuck there for ten more days – but like, fuck, would I have been upset to stay in this amazing city a little longer? Yeah, no!

The Guatemalan doctor greeted me at the hotel and quickly shoved a giant Q-Tip up my nose. Fortunately (or unfortunately), the 5-minute wait gave me a negative test result, and I was given a certificate to take with me to the airport.

The next 24 hours, though, would prove more unexpected than anything I could have prepared myself for.

The Fuckery that is...

A Motorcycle Ride.

"We travel not to escape life, but for life not to escape us."
– Anonymous

Joseph ran a couple errands while I got my test, and as I waited for him to pick me up, I got talking with Caleb, Herman, and Scott, three guys from NYC. I mentioned the Sky Café, and that'd I'd be meeting some friends there, tonight, if they wanted to join. As you've probably guessed, I'm kind of the nucleus when it comes to social gatherings, handing out verbal invites like candy. The guys agreed, just as Joseph pulled up on his bike.

I jumped on behind him, once again, and he whisked me away to his "office", which turned out to hold the bar, hotel, showroom, and tour company all in one. I plugged in my phone (fucking finally!) and Joseph gave me the tour of the place. The bar was definitely a biker joint, with eclectic photos and drawings plastered in no orderly fashion all over the walls. I'd even spotted a necklace hanging from a license plate behind the bar.

"I love that necklace," I said. "What's the story behind it?"

"Oh, nothing. I believe a girl who worked here a long time ago left it behind."

"Well, it's beautiful. You should come up with a better story!" I joked.

We walked through the showroom, which stored at least 20 motorbikes, all of which he owned as part of his tour company, MotoTours Guatemala. I wondered how many different people from all over the world had ridden these bikes throughout this wonderful country; and I felt a connection to this place, and to Joseph, with our shared entrepreneur lifestyles and motivation.

A couple entered the bar just as we sat down to have an ice-cold beer together.

"Hey, Kyle!" Joseph called. He introduced me to Kyle, a friend and colleague of his, and Kyle's gorgeous wife, Claudette. The four of us took our drinks and went up to the rooftop, as Joseph detailed every renovation he was planning for the space.

"It's so beautiful up here!" I said. "I have an idea. You should let me paint a mural around the terrace."

"Really? That would be awesome!"

"I guess I have to come back, then!"

Joseph seemed excited by that, and we talked about ideas for social media marketing, interior decorating, art, and ideas for promotions to get customers in his door. After all, I've been a marketing professional for over twenty years. I live for that shit!

***

When we got back downstairs, Joseph went over to the piano in the corner and asked if I knew how to play.

"I can, but only by ear. I've never had a lesson."

"I play by ear, too!"

"Okay, let me see what I can remember..."

I tried to jog my memory, plink-plonking the keys in the hopes my fingers would recall the Boyz II Men songs, or PM Dawn's *I'd Die Without You*, that I'd taught myself as a teenager. Needless to say, I failed miserably. I laughed at my failed attempt to impress him and settled on playing *Chopsticks*.

I wandered over to the bar check my phone's battery life, taking another sip of my beer as Joseph sat down at the piano. He played beautifully – really, I was shocked by how talented he was! – and I grabbed my phone to take a video.

At the end of the song, his head turned slightly in my direction, and his brown eyes gazed at me in a way that made a feeling of comfort settle deep in my bones. It felt as if, for just a moment, he was looking into my soul.

Fuck. Joseph and I had a connection – never mind that he wasn't my type at all. It was undeniable.

***

Later that day, Joseph offered to take me on a motorcycle ride through the mountains that neighbored Antigua.

"Hell yes!" I said – of course. I'd never one to back down from an adrenaline rush and a new adventure!

We hopped on his bike and headed out of the city, up through the twisty turns of the highly elevated roads. He'd made me feel safe enough when he'd driven me back to my hotel; but that was only a few blocks, and I was a little nervous that he'd turn into a daredevil show-off if he had free reign of the wheels over a longer distance. But I didn't feel scared – not even once.

The views were incredible, and the tiny neighborhoods we drove through were so poverty-stricken it hurt my heart. But this was the real Guatemala, that tourists don't really see. It was humbling and beautiful all at the same time. We stopped to take photos of beautiful churches and rolling mountain views, creating moments that will always stay with me. To be honest, not even the pictures could tell the story of those two hours as accurately as the memories imprinted on my heart.

***

We drove back down to the city to meet Erin at the Sky Café. I'd asked her to meet me around 4:00 PM, and I *hate* being late. As we climbed the stairs to the main-level restaurant, we found Tom, the sixty-something year old owner from Canada, sitting on a chair at the bar.

"Hey!" he said pleasantly. "How was the ride?"

"Oh my gosh, it was *awesome*! I can't believe I've never tried that, before!"

"Yeah, I really miss riding. That's how I lost my leg."

I gave him what I'm sure was the strangest look he's ever seen (keep in mind, one of my friends' favorite nicknames for me is "Faces".). "What?"

Tom swung one leg around the chair, showing that the other was, in fact, amputated well above the knee – something I hadn't noticed when we'd first met, hours prior.

 "What happened?" I asked, after a moment.

Tom told us how he'd gotten into a bad motorcycle accident less than a mile from his home. His left leg suffered over 14 fractures, and while the doctors attempted to save the injured limb, he got gangrene. We joked a bit about how that always seems to be the case, accidents happening so close to home; and I said I was kind of glad I didn't know about his accident prior to taking off on the bike with Joseph, as I may not have decided to go!

Tom laughed, handing Joseph and I a free beer each while we waited for Erin.

The Fuckery that is...

The Neverending Story.

"We don't even care whether or not we care." – Morla, The Neverending Story

Eventually, Erin arrived, and I introduced her to Joseph and Tom. We made our way up the narrow spiral staircase to the rooftop and grabbed a table. Joseph and Erin started chatting about her travels – mostly, how she'd planned to visit Semuc, an underground river about five hours outside of Antigua, but wouldn't have time. As it happened, Joseph was going to be leaving for Semuc the next day, and Erin promptly invited herself to join him.

Now, Joseph had already asked me to change my flight, to come with him on this weekend trip. I started to wonder if Erin was jealous, since Joseph was giving me most of his attention, and was obviously smitten with me.

At one point, I showed her a photo of a girlfriend of mine, who I thought she resembled.

"Hey, don't you think you two look alike?"

"Oh no, I hope I not!" Erin said, with a disgusted expression.

"Well, that's just rude. She's gorgeous!"

"What do you want me to say? You showed me some picture of a girl with your ex-husband!"

Not sure why *that* mattered. The girl was, in fact, an ex of my ex, but I hadn't meant anything by that. I'd simply meant to convey that they had similar qualities.

***

Caleb, Herman, and Scott had joined us at our table, slotting seamlessly into our conversation. Caleb and Scott mentioned that they were both married, while Herman was currently single.

Herman was very much my usual type, tall and handsome with strong facial features. Not *exactly* a Keanu Reeves lookalike, but he definitely gave off that vibe! I caught some flirty banter with him, exchanging Instagram follows so we could stay in touch about our plans; and I invited all the guys to come to La Taverna with us later. The more, the merrier!

***

Joseph had gone home to change, so it was just me and Erin on the road to La Taverna. We decided to swing by SKÅL for couple drinks while we waited for the guys, and were almost immediately roped into doing shots with a bunch of locals and fellow travelers. Liquor *really* isn't my thing, so I was pretty quick to decline when a tall, scruffy-looking German patron, sporting a blond man-bun, offered us whiskey and cocktails. Erin, however, clearly wasn't going to turn down free drinks of any kind!

I looked down at my phone to see a message from Joseph.

Hello! I am on my way back, where are you?
Hey! I replied. At SKÅL. Can you meet us here?

Another message popped up, this time from Herman.

Hey, what time should I meet you guys? Caleb and Scott are
staying behind, but I'd love to come out for some drinks!

I told him we'd be heading over to La Taverna soon, so he might
as well make his way there.

Herman's presence turned out to be a serious blessing for me
because once Joseph arrived and we went to La Taverna, Erin was
all over his nuts. She kept complaining about the bar being too
smoky and wanting to leave; but when Joseph didn't take the bait,
she still hung around. She got him to play a few rounds of darts
with her, all while I sat at the bar wondering what her deal was.

This previously great day was starting to feel like total bullshit.

Distracting myself from that scene, I talked with Herman about
our lives back in the States, confessing my love for Manhattan and
how I'd always wanted to live there and work for a big ad agency.
Herman, who was just 35, mentioned that while he had a good
career back home, he really wanted to travel the world.

"Funny you should say that" I said. "That's been my philosophy
for the last year or so! Well, the whole just living life, traveling,
being happy thing."

We had plenty of chat fuel in terms of travel experiences and places on our bucket lists, too. Honestly, I'd probably have left if Herman hadn't been there to keep me company.

Now, Joseph wasn't *completely* ignoring me. I caught him looking in my direction a few times, and he even came over to me to talk a bit here and there. That didn't do much to lessen the tension between Erin and I, though; and, after another couple hours, I decided enough was enough.

***

Joseph followed me outside, chased by some final, snarky remarks from Erin. He was supposed to be taking me back to my hotel, but, to my surprise, we rode back to his bar for a nightcap.

"What are we doing back here?" I asked.

"I have something for you."

Huh? Needless to say, I was intrigued.

We went inside. Joseph gave me a beer and lifted the necklace off the tattered license plate hanging on the wall.

"I want you to have this," he said, pressing it into my hand. "It's a new story."

His words, in that strange way words sometimes do, reminded me of that kooky fairytale movie from the 80s, *The Neverending Story*. An offhanded reference sparked a whole conversation: laughing, recalling our favorite parts, sharing memories of when we were kids and the impact it had on us. I told him I'd always thought the statues that shot lasers from their eyes had big boobs. He said he'd always wanted a flying dog just like Falkor.

"FALLLLKOOOOORR!" we both exclaimed simultaneously, followed by "ATRREEEYYYUUUU!", and my (rather pitiful) impression of the Childlike Empress saying, "Call my name!" Joseph started blasting the movie's theme song over the speakers. We busted out our best dance moves, yelling along to it – and, of course, I took a video of us belting out that iconic *"Never-ending storrrrryyyyyyy!"*.

We threw on track after track of our favorite music, continuing our two-person rave until well past 11:00 PM. He even played the piano for me again, this time *Nothing Else Matters* by Metallica – one of my top-five songs of all time thanks to its dark, moving lyrics.

I think we both knew what was about to happen, but I was still so timid about being touched, let alone kissed, after what I went through with Blake. It had been nearly nine months since I'd been intimate with anyone…

Joseph leaned into me. We kissed, softly. And for whatever crazy, unknown reason, I felt good about it. Hey, maybe this was just my moment to get back in the dick saddle!

What started as just a kiss turned passionate as all fucking get-out; and, before I knew it, we were going upstairs to his apartment. Once again, I had a moment of "what the fuck are you doing?" – I had to be up at 7:00 AM to catch my shuttle to the airport! – but, when it came down to it, I couldn't have given less of a shit.

***

One hour and three (or more!) of the best orgasms I've ever had later, Joseph drove me back to my hotel. He ended up staying in my room, where we had another round of amazing sex, slept, woke up, and went for round three – all in less than seven hours.

I was tired when I finally got up, but, fortunately, not hungover. I'd made sure to drink water and spread out the beer intake the night before so I wouldn't feel horrible on the flight (because let's face it, there is *nothing* worse than flying when you're hungover).

Joseph and I said our goodbyes as my taxi arrived. I loaded up my backpack and suitcase, and left Antigua.

The Fuckery that is...

Going Home.

"Speak your truth quietly and clearly; and listen to others, even the dull and ignorant; they too have their story." – Max Ehrmann, Desiderata (1927)

I had about two hours to kill at the airport in Guatemala City, so I sat down at the little bar close to my gate, pulled out my lavender-pink leather-bound journal, and started to write. I'd planned on writing much more throughout my trip, but I'd focused on seeing and doing as much as I possibly could, in the short six days I spent there, so I'd have more to write about! I also enjoyed one last authentic Gallo, the local Guatemalan brew.

***

The flight home felt all too quick. When I landed, I swear I felt a wave of sadness wash over me on the inside. Going back to my ordinary life, after this super high of solo travel, where I'd majorly restored my confidence in my independence, fucking sucked.

Shaun had jokingly texted me the week before I left, asking if I wanted a ride from the airport.

I'm a big girl! I'll get a Lyft or an Uber. Thanks so much, anyway!

I'd replied.

We'd been mostly just "bar buddies" except for that one morning on the beach and the ensuing trivia night – so imagine my surprise when I saw him waiting for me in arrivals! Perhaps our friendship had become more solid than I'd originally thought.

As soon as Shaun dropped me off at home, I hurried in to see Bula. She'd been staying with my next-door neighbor, Doug, while I was gone; and the moment I stepped in the door, she ran straight to my feet, butt wiggling like a bumblebee with a sugar rush, and began to love all over me. I'm pretty sure every time I leave with a suitcase, she thinks I'm never coming home.

I unpacked my suitcase – yes, I am one of those weird people who unpack immediately when I get home – then went over to Doug's so we could swap our travel stories. He'd gotten home from Michigan, where he'd visited for his son's wedding, the day I left for Guatemala.

After only an hour, I was restless.

You'd think after 24 hours of jumping between shuttles and planes, three hours of steaming-hot sex, barely any sleep, preceded by six days of gallivanting all over Guatemala, I'd be dead on my feet. But I had the urge to go somewhere, do something – because I had no intention of getting involved in the typical, drunken New Year's Eve festivities the following day.

I decided to make my way to Vega. At least the atmosphere there would take my mind off how I was feeling down and out.

Garza gave me a huge hug when I came in, and all my crappy feelings almost immediately melted away.

"So good to see you, my dear! How was your trip?"

"Oh my gosh, it was *everything*!" I said. "I'm kinda sad to be home."
"Oh, really? Tell me about it!"

I went into great detail about the churches, the ruins, Lake Atitlán, the Jesus exhibit that changed my life, and all the people I'd met. I even mentioned Joseph – how we'd had an amazing time, and eventually slept together.

Garza was very aware I still wasn't interested in dating anyone; but the look of surprise on his face when I told him I'd finally had sex with someone brought up some shame in me. I wasn't a one-night-stand type of girl, so I was debating going back to Antigua to see Joseph again and continue our discussions about marketing his businesses.

I didn't mean to hurt Garza, telling him about this, but I was going to be honest with him. I'd started to feel like maybe, just maybe, what I'd done with Joseph – arguably, while I was "on a break" (kind of like Ross and Rachel in *Friends*) – meant it was time for my relationship with myself to come to an end.

***

The next day was the last day of 2021. I spent time reflecting on everything I had been through that year: from Blake, to the new career, new city, loneliness and finding myself, being single on purpose, dating myself, and taking that solo trip. *So much...* I felt some anxiety at the thought, so I began writing and outlining plans for the year ahead.

I ordered in two pineapple, bacon, and pepperoni pizzas – one for me, and one for Doug – and headed next door with sustenance in hand, along with some crushed red pepper and honey. (Yes, I put honey on my pizza. It is fucking delicious.)

We settled down on Doug's dark-green leather couch with pink trim, ate some of that souped-up takeout, and watched the NYE show on TV. By 9:30 PM, I was home and curled up in bed for the night, checking out the messages and photos Joseph had sent me of his celebrations with his friends in Semuc. I thought that was sweet of him to get in touch; but I didn't think much more about it, at the time.

***

I slept exactly how I felt inside – like a fucking champion – ready to put all the brokenness behind me and continue my journey of healing. Similar to my 2020 moment, I woke up just once, right at 12:05 AM, to gently tap my finger on my phone and see that the new year had, in fact, begun.

I felt something so real deep down in my soul. 2022 was going to be the year of Ty.

The Fuckery that is...

Signs.

"Tolerance comes of age. I see no fault committed that I myself could not have committed at some time or other." – Johann Wolfgang von Goethe

I jumped out of bed at 6:00 AM, slathered some Preparation-H under my eyes to take the bags away, and drove out to the beach. What better way to start the year than to watch the very first sunrise from my very own sandbox that was just a mile from home?

To my surprise, there were tons of people there. You never saw crowds like this, here, unless it was noon on a 90-degree day! I managed to find a quiet-enough spot right where the sand met the ocean and took my usual seat on my flip flops. The sun rose without a cloud in the sky, and I had a BAC.

> **Belief:** A new year means a fresh start; the past no longer matters.
>
> **Action:** Make lists of things you'll resolve to do differently this year.
>
> **Challenge:** This sunrise is just like every other sunrise. It's another new day, not just a new year. Yesterday is still yesterday. Tomorrow is still tomorrow. Every day can be treated no differently than how society treats a new year.

Anything would be possible, if I made daily lists of the things I wanted to accomplish and stuck to them. Setting a daily goal was just as important as setting bigger goals, because small tasks would add up; and, while the past would still hold a place in my life, just because it was a new year wouldn't mean I'd forget everything that shaped me.

***

I'd already read Gabrielle Stone's book *Eat, Pray, #FML*, before leaving for Guatemala. I finished it in less than two days, and immediately ordered the sequel, *The Ridiculous Misadventures of a Single Girl.*

Her unbelievable stories above love, loss, and heartbreak, as well as her travels and adventures, inspired me to start writing the book you're now holding.

Admittedly, I didn't read as much as I'd planned while I was on my solo trip; and, although I was feeling inspired to write, I wanted to finish what I'd started, first. So, I made a goal for myself, that day, to spend at least a good few hours with that book. I got home from the beach around 7:45 AM, sat on my balcony with Bula and a cup of coffee, and just *read*, taking notes on anything that resonated with me so I could keep my creative fire burning.

Sometime during the late afternoon, my phone began to vibrate. I saw *Joseph would like to video chat* on the screen, set the book aside, and answered.

"Hey!" I took a quick look at myself in the little on-screen window above his handsome face – a long enough look to think, *Oh, for fuck's sake, Ty, you look like shit!* I hadn't yet showered, and was still in my Detroit Lions sweatpants, a tank top, and no makeup with my hair in a low-effort ponytail.

"Hi, Ty! Great to see you again, you look beautiful!"

Now, Joseph appeared to be a few stiff drinks into his Saturday, so I figured he probably had some beer goggles on when he told me that. But I still felt a little twinkle inside. Who wouldn't have? Sure, I wasn't 100% on where Joseph and I stood – whether this was a real connection, or just some vacation ass, another random piece in life's ever-changing puzzle – but I wanted to find out!

***

I spent my entire Sunday, from 7:00 AM until 10:00 PM reading and taking more notes. In a chapter called "Accepting the Signs", Gabrielle talked about meeting a girl who'd been in a motorbike accident. Well, how about that? I'd literally just been on a motorcycle for the very first time in my life days prior, with Joseph. *Weird...*

I turned a few more pages, and, lo and be-fucking-hold, she mentioned *The Neverending Story*. Now that was downright crazy. Before Joseph had brought it up, I hadn't even thought about the damn movie in – oh, twenty or so years? And now, not even four days after we'd been singing and dancing to the theme song, and reciting lines from the script, it's *right here*, staring me in the face?

Was this... a *sign?*

Not even three minutes later, my phone beeped with a WhatsApp notification. No surprise, it was Joseph.

We messaged each other for a bit; and, just as he arrived back home from Semuc, he video-called me for a second time.

The Fuckery that is...

A One-Night Stand.

"Sometimes I think I think too much. Sometimes I think I don't think enough. Then I think about why I think I'm thinking about it at all." – Ty Paige

I went back to work on Monday; and, while I never expected for my phone to be blown up with messages all day, I thought I'd probably hear from Joseph at some point. Alas, there was nothing.

He finally texted me – after I'd come home, taken Bula for a walk, and started dinner.

Hi beautiful! I'll call you tonight when I get to bed.

And so, hours later, I slid into my green-and-white chevron patterned sheets, wearing a tank top and panties, pulled my multi-color floral comforter over me, and waited.

And waited.

And waited…

Eventually, I had to accept that I wasn't going to hear from him that night. BAC time!

Belief: When someone says they are going to do something, they do it.

Action: You expect that others will do what you would do, so you feel disappointed and sad. You must not matter.

Challenge: Don't wait around for anyone to follow through on a promise. People are not always reliable, and just because you'd follow through doesn't mean they will.

***

Two days later, I sent Erin a message. I hadn't checked in with her since she'd left Guatemala for her next adventure in Costa Rica. I had always been the type to let bygones be bygones, and plus, I'd had way more fun with her throughout the trip than with anyone else I'd met (other than Joseph, for obvious reasons!).

Hey Erin! How is Costa Rica?

Hey girl, OMG I love it here. How are you?

Sad to be home, but I'm doing okay. Back to work and reality!

Why sad? She asked.

I think I'll go back to Guatemala soon to see Joseph, we've been talking ever since I left.

Wait.

Erin is typing...

A photo appeared: a screenshot of a message thread between her and Joseph from the day I left. Joseph had told her he thought I was weird and asked her to coffee or dinner.

Oh my God. When was that? I asked.

Just saying I care for your heart, and he is a flirt, be careful.

I thanked her for being so transparent with me – I fucking love it when girls stick together! I knew there must have been a reason, even after that night when things got awkward between Erin and I, that I'd followed up with her.

I sent the photo to Joseph shortly after. He tried to tell me he meant to say "it" was weird – but the letters were clear as day. *Ty was weird.* He also said he'd made that offer to Erin because they'd made a bet when they were playing darts, and he was just following through on it. He even recorded a voice message telling me he was sorry, he really liked me, and could we put this behind us. I didn't believe him.

Here we go, another BAC.

> **Belief:** He apologized, he is sorry. He didn't really mean to say your name – maybe he mistyped, or got mixed up, since English is his second language.
>
> **Action:** Let it go. It was nothing. You don't even really know him, anyway.
>
> **Challenge:** "Being a good person" is a universal language. Read it again, Ty. He called you weird. Don't justify his inappropriate behavior. Fuck that.

I turned off my WhatsApp notifications – I barely used it, anyway, before I went to Guatemala. I tucked myself into bed, telling myself he was just vacation ass, I was just tourist ass, and "signs" are bullshit.

It was just a one-night stand, and I had no regrets.

The Fuckery that is...

The Unknown.

"Time does not determine the strength of any love, it is what happens during that time that does." – Ty Paige

Just one week into the new year, I'd already committed to writing every single day. Some days, I'd manage 2,000 words; others, I'd crank out over 10,000. I posted my progress to my social media accounts, where friends and strangers alike reached out to me with inspiring and uplifting words. The amount of encouragement I received from close friends I'd known my whole life, newer friends I'd only known just a few years, and even people I'd only met once or twice, was overwhelming.

I kept writing, and I kept feeling: abandonment, rejection, fear, disappointment, betrayal, and disregard; satisfaction, love, support, faith, inspiration, devotion – and, most of all, *independence*. I came to terms with the fact that my entire life had been complicated by love, something that's supposed to be simple. Perhaps that was because I'd never learned, before, that self-love comes first.

Having spent almost a year, now, prioritizing myself, I've stopped worrying about things I can't control. I feel more secure in my life than ever before, and in my body, my clothes, my decisions, my art, my writing, my imperfections… and my story.

***

I don't know what will happen in my next book. Shit, I still don't know why the Santa Catalina Arch resonated with me so much. But you know what? That's okay. Sometimes, we aren't meant to know the whys, hows, or whats of life – even when we walk in it, around it, and through it twice a day.

The next step in my journey is a week-long solo trip to Colombia. Then, of course, write the fucking sequel.

I will also publish two journals – the first, "F*ck You, Watch Me Love Myself" for adults, and a second titled, "I can. I will. Watch This." for teenagers who've had rough upbringings. For every adult journal sold, I will donate a teen journal to various troubled youth organizations.

And maybe ask Garza to go on a date.

This story began with the desire to have the true love of a man – and ends with the true love of a Moza: me.

The Fuckery that is...

Not Fuckery.

The Epilogue

"There is no greater agony than bearing an untold story inside you."
-Maya Angelou.

Firstly, and most importantly: if you or someone you know is experiencing domestic violence, or is in an otherwise abusive relationship, please reach out to a crisis hotline.

In the US, you can contact the National Domestic Violence Hotline in the following ways:

Call: **1-800-799-SAFE**
Text: **"START" to 88788**
Search: **www.thehotline.org***

Stay safe and stay strong. If I can do it, you can too.

Secondly: this journey to choosing myself over a man was not an easy one. I still want to find a companion one day. Only God knows who he is and where he is; but he will not be a from-the-ground-up project, or even a fixer-upper. When I think of my next relationship, it manifests a lot like a tree. It will have deep roots, branches of trust, but will always (of course) need a little upkeep. It will be strong, free-standing, and continuously blossom, and no amount of external force will ever take it down.

I ask God all the time for strength, guidance, discipline, motivation, and forgiveness. Whether you're religious and pray, or if that's just not your thing, you can tell yourself that you, too, are capable of living your life with SGDM.

And forgiveness. Without forgiveness, I would not be where I am today. I've forgiven everyone in my past who has hurt me, and I've forgiven myself for making poor choices like a crazy, insecure girl desperate for reassurance and acceptance. As soon as you decide you want to take yourself on the journey of self-love, let go of all the mistakes in your life. Once you do that, you can start challenging your impetuous beliefs and reinventing them to be your core beliefs. And once you accept your new core beliefs, you will start to act on them.

Just remember to take a deep breath, close your eyes, shake up the snow globe with the fierceness of *everything* you are, watch those bullshit belief snowflakes swirl around… then throw it with all your might at a tree.

Acknowledgments.

Michalle, Sue, Liz, Sam, Kelly, Allie, Kristin, Laron, Erin, Jessica, James & Kelly, Linda, Theresa, Jason. Countless others, you *all* know who you are.

You guys *are* my family and I love you more than 61,455 words can describe.

Thank you to so many amazing people near and far for never giving up on me, always encouraging me, and allowing me to take this journey to loving my silly self without judgment.

Thanks to Megan Openshaw with MLO Proofreading. Your work is nothing short of fucking awesome. My book would not be what it is without your talent.

Thank you, Colin McConnell, for the most fun photoshoot I have ever had. Destroying my dress and capturing the therapy on film was not only awesome – but made my book cover!

Thank you to Courtney Olbrich for being my very first friend to read my un-edited manuscript and give honest feedback.

Love.

The words of encouragement I have received throughout my journey to self-love have changed my life forever. Guys, go be great, and lift each up other always. <3

Sue O. wrote:

You're an amazing strong badass woman! I'm so proud of you, just wanted to let you know. I love seeing you win!

Lisa wrote:

Happy New Year! I just wanted to let you know what an incredible person you are. You inspire me to take chances and let my soul lead the way. I stalk your travel adventures! You burn so bright, keep shining!

Ashley G. wrote:

So proud of you for going on a huge solo trip! Proud of you for writing your book, that is a huge accomplishment.

Kimmy wrote:

I love you and I love seeing your post and your journey and I am so happy you are happy!

Mandy wrote:

You are so very inspiring! I will read your book!

Kelly T. wrote:

You are one of the sweetest, most genuine women I have ever known. Anyone who mistreats you is not worth your time anyway. You do you, girl. Loving yourself looks amazing on you!

Michelle wrote:

I loved you the first day I met you. I've always known how special you are. It's funny how that happens. Within one conversation you made me believe so much is possible.

Christy wrote:

I love you! And wow, what an incredible woman you are inside and out!!

Ashley K. wrote:

I've only ever met you one time, in a bar on a snowy day in the middle of Nebraska... I've admired you ever since then. Not stalkerish, but every time I see your posts you motivate me to do more and step out and live life. Thank you for sitting by me on that bar stool that one time.

Lindsay wrote:

You are beautiful and amazing inside and out!! I love watching how strong you have become. It has definitely inspired me! Keep doing you!

Melissa G. wrote:

You are easily one of the sweetest and most genuine people I've encountered... two seconds into talking to you and your kind heart shines through. Keep doing you... you're inspiring so many of us to become better versions of ourselves.

Brett G. wrote:

I'm so happy for you!!! Proud to be able to say I know you!!! You don't know how much you encourage people, just by living your life!! Keep it up!!! FUWATCHTHIS!

Kris Ann Wrote:

Ty, you have always been one of my very favorites, going way, way back, with a beautiful heart, determination, and quite an inspiration to those who are secure enough within themselves of see. It's music to my ears to see you've chosen yourself, as God created one amazing shining star when he made you. Congratulations on your book, I'm looking forward to reading.

I fucking love you guys.

Resources.

A Rejoyceful Animal Rescue
www.rejoycefulrescue.com

MotoTours Guatemala
www.mototours-guatemala.com

Gabrielle Stone
Author of *Eat, Pray, #FML* and *The Ridiculous Misadventures of a Single Girl.*
www.eatprayfml.com

Little Angel Gowns
www.littleangelgowns.org

MLO Proofreading
www.mloproofreading.com

Colin McConnell Photography
Instagram: @colindetroit

Girls LOVE Travel®
www.facebook.com/groups/GirlsLoveTravel

F*CK YOU
Watch This.

SOCIALLY YOURS

#FUWatchThis
@FUWatchThis
@tylarpaige
fuwatchthis.com

www.ingramcontent.com/pod-product-compliance
Lightning Source LLC
Chambersburg PA
CBHW062119020426
42335CB00013B/1024